The SURVIVAL KIT
Family Haggadah

Shimon Apisdorf

LEVIATHAN PRESS
BOOKS THAT MAKE A DIFFERENCE

The Survival Kit Family Haggadah
by Shimon Apisdorf
published by

2505 Summerson Road Baltimore, Maryland 21209
1-800-LEVIATHAN

ISBN 1-881927-11-3

Printed in the United States of America / First Printing
Cover illustration by Julius Ciss (416) 784-1416
Cover and jacket design by Lightbourne Images
Page layout by Fisherman Sam
Hebrew typography by Mendelsohn Press
The Matzahbrei Family by Bill Hackney of Staiman Design
Distributed to the trade by NBN (800) 462-6420

Group Sales: Leviathan Press books are available to schools,
synagogues, businesses and community organizations at special
group rates. Customized books on a per order basis are also
available. Titles include: The Chanukah Revival Kit, The One
Hour Purim Primer, Passover Survival Kit, The Survival Kit
Family Haggadah, Rosh Hashanah Yom Kippur Survival Kit,
Missiles, Masks And Miracles and The Death of Cupid:
Reclaiming the wisdom of love, dating, romance and marriage.
For information call (410) 653-0300.

In appreciation of
your commitment
and involvement with
THE ASSOCIATED…

Thanks for all you do!

Chag Sameach

Howard E. Friedman
General Campaign Chair

Ronnie Glaser
Women's Department
Campaign Chair

campaign 2000

community. caring.

THE ASSOCIATED
JEWISH COMMUNITY FEDERATION OF BALTIMORE

COMMITMENT.

The author would like to acknowledge the following ...

APPRECIATION

Donna Cohen, Rabbi Michel & Rebbetzin Feige Twerski, Oscar Rosenberg, Barry, Rita, Jacquelyn & Jason, Sam Glazer, Yehudis Silverstein, Shlomo & Dori Horwitz, Goldie Lurie, Rabbi Yaacov & Rebbetzin Chana Weinberg, Reuven, Jenny & Binyomin Aharon, Ann Sinclair, Auntie, Ann Apisdorf, Rabbi Asher Resnick, Yechezkal Mordechai Nemani, Russell & Julie, The one and only Uncle Harry, Leslie & Zoe, George Rohr, Yaacov Levitz, Julie Starkoff, Josh & Amy, Lisa, Dr. Bill & Eleanor Eisner, Scott & Shelley Israel, Sherri Cohen, Avi Waxman, Arthur Rosenthal, Ciaran Mercier, PMA, NBN and my favorite inner child, Sammy Matzahbrei.

SPECIAL THANKS

My parents, David and Bernice Apisdorf. When I need parents, they are there. When I need friends, they are there. When I need advice, they are there.

Mr. and Mrs. Robert and Charlotte Rothenburg. May they be blessed with good health and much nachas.

Esther Rivka, Ditzah Leah and Yitzchak Ben Zion. Three shining lights who make every seder, and every day, a gift to be cherished forever.

My wife Miriam. The most important things in life I learn from you. Love, prayer, honesty, perseverance, kindness, maturity, No LH and the power of humor.

DEDICATION

This Haggadah is dedicated to Rabbi Noah & Rebbetzin Deena Weinberg. If I and my family have merited to share a bit of the beauty of Jewish life with others, it is only because we in turn benefitted from the dedication and teaching of the Weinbergs.

Everything is possible only because of the Almighty's blessings: And with those blessings, anything is possible. Next Year in Jerusalem.

Praise for other books by Shimon Apisdorf

Passover Survival Kit
Rosh Hashanah Yom Kippur Survival Kit   Bestselling winner
of the Benjamin Franklin Award
The One Hour Purim Primer: Everything a family needs to
understand, celebrate and enjoy Purim.
The Death Of Cupid: Reclaiming the wisdom of love, dating,
romance and marriage. By Nachum Braverman and Shimon
Apisdorf (Spring 1997)
The Chanukah Revival Kit (Fall 1997)

*"The relevance of the Passover Seder comes to life with this excel-
lent, well written guide."*
                                        Detroit Jewish News

*"Apisdorf understands the heartbeat of our generation with
incomparable clarity; he knows where it hurts and what to do
about it."*
                        Rabbi Michel and Rebbetzin Feige Twerski

*"Apisdorf gets out the deeper meaning behind the stock answers
to "why is this night different from all other nights." His clear
style cuts through layers of built-up boredom to uncover a fresh-
ness we hardly imagined could exist."*
                                        Ohio Jewish Chronicle

*"He has a unique ability to communicate the practical wisdom
of Judaism and show how it relates to everyday life in the
modern world."*
                                        The Jerusalem Report

*"People who usually spend High Holy Day services
counting the ceiling tiles will sit up and pay attention."*
                                        Baltimore Jewish Times

*"For ordinary Jews, the Rosh Hashanah Yom Kippur Survival
Kit is, quite literally a god-send."*
                                        Kansas City Jewish Chronicle

*"I wish I had this book 25 years ago. The Death of Cupid is a
must for anyone who wants to stay happily married."*
                                        Larry King, CNN

The **SURVIVAL KIT**
Family Haggadah

Welcome to the Seder.

Hi, my name is Ira Matzahbrei, and it's my pleasure to welcome you to The Survival Kit Family Haggadah. We are going to be spending a lot of time together tonight, and I want to take this opportunity to encourage you to relax and do whatever you need to make this seder an enjoyable and meaningful one. In fact, that's what makes this Haggadah so special. You see, we know that the seder can be a very challenging experience; that the text of the Haggadah can be hard to follow, that some of the rituals might seem a bit odd, and that frankly, the whole thing can turn into a bit of a drag. So what we've done is build into this Haggadah an assortment of aids that are designed to help you access the wonderful potential that exists within the seder.

Before we get into the seder itself, I want you to meet the rest of my family. Each member of the Matzahbrei family has a special role to play in the seder tonight. After meeting the family, you will be offered some tips on how to best use this Haggadah. I encourage you to read the rest of this introduction carefully. I'll see you later on page nineteen where the seder begins.

MEET THE MATZAHBREI FAMILY

My name is Miriam Matzahbrei. In addition to taking care of my family, I also teach philosophy at our local Jewish day school. My students call me Morah Miriam, but you can call me Miriam.

My job at the seder tonight is to share insights with you that are hidden within the text of the Haggadah. The ideas that I will be sharing have been chosen because they show how the message of the Haggadah can be relevant to our lives today. Of course, not every insight will seem relevant to everyone at the seder, however I do hope that there are at least a few that each person can relate to.

I want to join my husband in welcoming you to The Survival Kit Family Haggadah, and I want to wish you all a healthy, happy and insightful seder.

Hi, I'm Rebecca Matzahbrei. Whenever you see me tonight, you will know that there is something to read that will be of particular interest to children. After all, us kids are supposed to be the center of attention at the seder. For this reason, The Survival Kit Family Haggadah has been very careful to incorporate explanations and mini-essays that kids can read and discuss.

See you later, and have a great seder.

Hi, I'm Sammy, and my job tonight is to have fun. I'm excited that we are all together and I just know that we are going to have a great time. See you at the ten plagues!

ABOUT THE "TALKING HAGGADAH"

The Survival Kit Family Haggadah contains two texts of the Haggadah. One text is the traditional hebrew text. If you can read and understand hebrew, that's great, by all means use the hebrew. Tonight however, since most people are far more comfortable with english than hebrew, The Survival Kit Family Haggadah will use the **Talking Haggadah** translation as it's primary text.

The **Talking Haggadah** translation is not a literal translation of the Haggadah. The **Talking Haggadah** is a unique translation that adheres very closely to the meaning of the original text, but at the same time, incorporates background information, clarifications and explanations into the text itself. It also uses words and language that are more like the way most people talk today. You won't find any "Thees" or "Thous" in this Haggadah.

The goal of the **Talking Haggadah** translation is to make an often cumbersome text easy to read and understand. In addition to the translation, Ira Matzahbrei will provide further clarification of the Haggadah where he feels it is necessary.

THE PASSOVER SURVIVAL KIT

The Survival Kit Family Haggadah has a companion volume called, the *Passover Survival Kit*. Throughout The Survival Kit Family Haggadah, you will find this symbol. This is used to indicate that if you want to find out more about what is taking place at that particular point in the seder, then all you have to do is look in the *Passover Survival Kit* on the page that appears in the box.

SOME FUN IDEAS

Passover is for kids!

There is an ancient custom to spread nuts on the seder table before the seder begins. And what is the deep, hidden meaning behind this custom? Simply, to arouse the curiosity of the children at the seder.

There is also the well known, time honored custom of hiding the afikomen and letting the children hunt for it. Again, another custom designed to keep children involved in the seder.

The following list contains a number of ideas that will help to stimulate the involvement of children at the seder.

1) For a couple of weeks before Passover, try reading Passover stories with your kids at night. It is also a good idea to find a book about Passover which can be read at the dinner table every night as Passover approaches.

1a) Based on what you have read with your children, you can now ask questions at the seder that they will be able to answer. This excites them, makes them feel good about themselves, and is a wonderful source of *nachas* for the grandparents. You can have little prizes to give out for correct answers. After a while, you will see that the adults will want prizes too. Go ahead, it's part of the fun. Caution: Be sensitive to the children of guests. Find ways to include them too.

1b) In case you didn't have a chance to do this before Passover, we have included a section that appears intermittently throughout the Haggadah called, **Fun Facts**. This section contains questions about Passover, the story of the Jews in Egypt, and about some of the basics of Judaism. This section provides a great way for everyone, adults included, to learn a lot of important information that is relevant to Passover. (Answers to all the questions appear on page 97.)

The leader of the seder can ask the questions as they appear in the Haggadah and give prizes, candy or other treats for every correct answer. Also, every time someone gets a correct answer they can be given a nut or a toothpick. Whoever has the most nuts at the end of the seder wins a grand prize.

1c) Good questions deserve just as much recognition as good answers. Anytime someone asks a good question about the Haggadah or the seder, they should be rewarded and encouraged to keep up the good work.

2) A short skit.

Write a short skit about the exodus from Egypt. Characters can include Moses, Pharaoh, God, a firstborn Egyptian, a Jewish slave, an Egyptian taskmaster, a frog, etc. Short written scripts can be given to each child (adults too if they want). Give the kids your full attention—remember; tonight they are the stars of the show.

3) Find the patterns.

The number four is significant on Passover and there are numerous instances of things appearing in groupings and patterns of four throughout the Haggadah. Every time someone notices a pattern of four, give them a toothpick. The one with the most toothpicks at the end of the seder gets a prize. Try to find a way to make everyone a winner—we certainly don't want anyone to feel like a loser on Passover.

4) Sticker madness.

Jewish bookstores carry a variety of colorful Passover stickers. These can be a lot of fun when incorporated into the seder as prizes for asking or answering a question, noticing a pattern, or reading a paragraph in the Haggadah. They can also be used to keep the children excited about fulfilling the mitzvot at the seder. When they eat matzah, they get a matzah sticker, for maror they get a bitter herb sticker, and so on. (Sammy likes the stickers with the wobbly eyes the best.)

5) The ten plagues.

The ten plagues provide a great opportunity to do all sorts of great stuff at the seder. Long before Passover, you can start a collection of visual aids for the ten plagues. Some examples:

Blood— Wrap red cellophane paper around a glass. When you pour water into the glass, you suddenly have a glass of blood. Pour water from the glass into a clear cup, and the water is now crystal clear. This is exactly what happened in Egypt; the same water that was bloody in the glass of an Egyptian, was clear and drinkable for a Jew.

Frogs & Locusts— There are a wide variety of frogs and locusts available at the nature store in your local shopping mall.

Hail— Ping pong balls make for great hail.

Wild animals— You can buy all sorts of plastic animals and toss them out on the table. You can also buy masks and become an animal, or you can have different kids (and adults too) play the part of a particular animal.

Pestilence— Just turn your plastic animals on their backs and presto—dead animals.

Darkness— Pass out dark sunglasses to everyone at the seder.

There are only two rules when it comes to the ten plagues: Be creative, and have lots of fun!

A COMMENT ABOUT THE COMMENTARY

The goal of The Survival Kit Family Haggadah commentary is to enable people to discover, within the text of the Haggadah, ideas, inspirations and insights that relate to life as it is lived every day. The Haggadah not only chronicles the historical birth of the Jewish nation, but it also contains seminal ideas that are basic to a Jewish understanding of life in general, Jewish life in particular and most particularly, the issue of freedom in our lives.

Passover is known as *Z'man Cheyrutaynu*, The Season of Freedom. The themes of national, personal, spiritual and emotional freedom are all woven together in the text of the Haggadah. The commentary in this Haggadah is an attempt to reveal some of those themes.

The commentary is divided into two parts: Questions & Answers, and Mini-Essays. The Question & Answer portion of the commentary tries to anticipate questions about the Haggadah text, and then present insightful answers. The children of the Haggadah; the wise child, the rebellious child and the simple child, each pose questions from their particular perspective. The Mini-Essays come in two forms: Those that are written especially for children (Rebecca is usually in charge of these), and others that are on a more adult level (Miriam Matzahbrei will often present these).

It is important to keep in mind that one need not read the entire commentary during the seder. As a matter of fact, you can skip the whole thing if you want and just stick to the basic text of the Haggadah. The commentary is intended to enhance your experience of the seder. It can be read at the seder, in full or in part, or it can be read either before Passover in preparation for the seder, or sometime after the seder as a way to reflect more deeply on what you have experienced.

RELAX AND ENJOY

The Passover Seder is not supposed to be a race, a test of endurance or a Jewish tribal right of passage. The seder is meant to be an enjoyable and enlightening experience where families and friends celebrate their Jewish identity; attempt to understand that identity a little better, and try to communicate the richness of Jewish life to the next generation.

Again: THIS IS NOT A TEST.

The ideal environment for a seder is one where people are comfortable and relaxed, where people feel free to participate or not, where no question is too simple and where everyone feels that they can learn, share and grow together.

So remember: Relax, take your time, learn, enjoy, grow and enjoy your seder; your celebration of being a part of the Jewish people.

And if things don't go exactly the way you hoped they would, hey, that's okay; because there is always next year—in Jerusalem!

THE SEDER PLATE

The seder plate, along with matzah and the four cups of wine, is one of the most recognizeable items at the seder. Every seder plate, no matter how simple or elaborate, is comprised of the same ten items.

21
PSK

The ten items of the seder plate are:
Matzah (three whole matzahs)
Z'roa (a roasted bone)
Beitzah (a roasted egg)
Maror (bitter herbs; like horseradish root or romaine lettuce)
Charoset (chopped almonds, apple, cinnamon and wine)
Karpas (a vegetable; like parsley, potato or celery)
Chazeret (a second vegetable or bitter herb)
K'arah (the seder plate itself)

THE SEDER BEGINS HERE

The seder actually begins with Kadesh (Kiddush) on the next page, however, it is customary to begin with a recitation of the various parts of the seder. This is kind of like taking a good look at a road map before you leave for a trip.

From beginning to end, the seder is comprised of fifteen specific experiences. These fifteen segments of the seder follow a precise order, and each comes with it's own set of instructions. Before proceeding to kiddush, the blessing over the first of the four cups of wine, everyone sings or reads together the list of the fifteen seder observances.

1. **Kadesh** A special blessing is recited over a glass of wine or grape juice. This blessing speaks of the treasured role that all holidays play in Jewish life, and makes particular reference to the unique opportunity embodied in Passover.
2. **Urechatz** Before eating the karpas, everyone washes their hands in the prescribed manner. Unlike the washing before the matzah, no blessing is said at this point.
3. **Karpas** A piece of vegetable is dipped in salt water and eaten.
4. **Yachatz** The middle matzah is broken in half. The larger half becomes the afikomen.
5. **Maggid** The reading and discussion of the Haggadah text.
6. **Rachtzah** Washing the hands before eating matzah. A blessing is recited after washing ones hands.
7. **Motzi** The blessing said anytime one eats bread or matzah.
8. **Matzah** A blessing is said, and a piece of matzah is eaten.
9. **Maror** A blessing is said, and the bitter herbs are eaten.
10. **Korech** Having just eaten matzah and bitter herbs separately, we now eat them together as a sandwich.
11. **Shulchan Orech** The festive Passover meal is enjoyed by all.
12. **Tzafon** The afikomen, which had been hidden earlier, is now brought back and everyone eats a piece of matzah as their own personal afikomen.
13. **Barech** The Birkat Hamazon blessing is said at the conclusion of the meal.
14. **Hallel** Reciting the songs of praise authored by King David.
15. **Nirtzah** The conclusion of the seder.

57
פסח

KADESH (KIDDUSH)

You are about to begin your seder, and that's exciting. However, before you begin, make sure to do whatever is necessary to make your guests comfortable. First of all, make sure that everyone knows who everyone else is. As the host and leader of the seder, you may want to go around the table, mention everyone's name, and in a sentence or two tell them why you are glad they are here. Also, be sure to tell people to relax and make themselves at home.

Passover is the Festival of Freedom, and tonight every Jew is supposed to feel as free as a king or a queen. For this reason one is required to recline at certain times during the seder. Also, to enhance this feeling of freedom, there is a custom for people to have a pillow at their chairs to make the reclining easy and comfortable. It is quite appropriate to offer your guests a pillow if they would like one.

Well, let's begin, and God willing we will all have an enjoyable seder.

The seder should begin, and kiddush should be recited, as soon after nightfall as possible. We wait until nighttime so that the entire seder takes place when it is actually Passover—which occurs with nightfall—yet we begin as early as feasible to facilitate the involvement of the children.

Kiddush is the first of the four cups. Each person's cup should be poured by someone else. This is how it's done for royalty, and tonight we are all members of a royal family.

On Friday night begin kiddush here.

And there was evening and there was morning; The sixth day. The heaven and the earth were completed, and all that they contained. On the seventh day God completed His work which He had done, and He abstained on the seventh day from all His work which He had made. God blessed the seventh day and sanctified it; because on it He abstained from all His work which God created to make.

Kiddush begins here. On Friday night include words in parentheses.

Blessed are You, Adonai, our God, King of the universe, Who creates the fruit of the vine.

בָּרוּךְ אַתָּה יְהֹוָה אֱלֹהֵינוּ מֶלֶךְ הָעוֹלָם, בּוֹרֵא פְּרִי הַגָּפֶן:

Baruch attah Adonai, eloheynu melech ha-olam, boray p'ri ha-gafen.

Blessed are You, Adonai, our God, King of the universe, Who has chosen us from all nations, who has exalted us above all tongues, and sanctified us with His commandments. And You, Adonai, our God, have given us in love (Sabbaths for rest), specially appointed times for gladness, feasts and seasons for

joy, (this Sabbath and) this Festival of Matzos, the time of our freedom (in love), a holy gathering to remember the Exodus from Egypt. For You have chosen us and sanctified us above all nations, (and the Sabbath) and Your holy festivals (in love and favor), in gladness and joy You have granted us our identity; our heritage. Blessed are You, Adonai, Who sanctifies (the Sabbath,) the Jewish People (Israel), and the festive seasons.

Kiddush concludes with the following blessing.

Blessed are You, Adonai, our God, King of the universe, Who has kept us alive, sustained us, and brought us to this specific time.

בָּרוּךְ אַתָּה יְהוָה אֱלֹהֵינוּ מֶלֶךְ הָעוֹלָם, שֶׁהֶחֱיָנוּ וְקִיְּמָנוּ וְהִגִּיעָנוּ לַזְּמַן הַזֶּה:

Baruch attah Adonai, eloheynu melech ha-olam, sheh-heh-che-yanu, ve-kiy'manu, ve-higi-anu la-z'man ha-zeh.

The wine should be drunk while reclining on the left side. It is preferable to drink the entire cup, but at the very least, one should drink most of the cup.

יוֹם הַשִּׁשִּׁי: וַיְכֻלּוּ הַשָּׁמַיִם וְהָאָרֶץ וְכָל־צְבָאָם: וַיְכַל אֱלֹהִים בַּיּוֹם הַשְּׁבִיעִי מְלַאכְתּוֹ אֲשֶׁר עָשָׂה, וַיִּשְׁבֹּת בַּיּוֹם הַשְּׁבִיעִי מִכָּל־מְלַאכְתּוֹ אֲשֶׁר עָשָׂה: וַיְבָרֶךְ אֱלֹהִים אֶת־יוֹם הַשְּׁבִיעִי וַיְקַדֵּשׁ אֹתוֹ, כִּי בוֹ שָׁבַת מִכָּל־מְלַאכְתּוֹ אֲשֶׁר־בָּרָא אֱלֹהִים לַעֲשׂוֹת:

בָּרוּךְ אַתָּה יְהוָה אֱלֹהֵינוּ מֶלֶךְ הָעוֹלָם, בּוֹרֵא פְּרִי הַגָּפֶן:

בָּרוּךְ אַתָּה יְהוָה אֱלֹהֵינוּ מֶלֶךְ הָעוֹלָם, אֲשֶׁר בָּחַר־בָּנוּ מִכָּל־עָם, וְרוֹמְמָנוּ מִכָּל־לָשׁוֹן, וְקִדְּשָׁנוּ בְּמִצְוֹתָיו. וַתִּתֶּן־לָנוּ יְהוָה אֱלֹהֵינוּ בְּאַהֲבָה (שַׁבָּתוֹת לִמְנוּחָה וּ) מוֹעֲדִים לְשִׂמְחָה, חַגִּים וּזְמַנִּים לְשָׂשׂוֹן, אֶת־יוֹם (הַשַּׁבָּת הַזֶּה וְאֶת־יוֹם) חַג הַמַּצּוֹת הַזֶּה, זְמַן חֵרוּתֵנוּ (בְּאַהֲבָה) מִקְרָא קֹדֶשׁ, זֵכֶר לִיצִיאַת מִצְרָיִם. כִּי בָנוּ בָחַרְתָּ וְאוֹתָנוּ קִדַּשְׁתָּ מִכָּל־הָעַמִּים, (וְשַׁבָּת) וּמוֹעֲדֵי קָדְשֶׁךָ (בְּאַהֲבָה וּבְרָצוֹן) בְּשִׂמְחָה וּבְשָׂשׂוֹן הִנְחַלְתָּנוּ: בָּרוּךְ אַתָּה יְהוָה מְקַדֵּשׁ (הַשַּׁבָּת וְ) יִשְׂרָאֵל וְהַזְּמַנִּים: בָּרוּךְ אַתָּה יְהוָה אֱלֹהֵינוּ מֶלֶךְ הָעוֹלָם שֶׁהֶחֱיָנוּ וְקִיְּמָנוּ וְהִגִּיעָנוּ לַזְּמַן הַזֶּה:

KIDDUSH

Many of your favorite places don't look anything like your house, your neighborhood or your school. Maybe you love the zoo. Or maybe you have a favorite museum or amusement park, or maybe you have been to Disney World.

Places like zoos and aquariums and amusement parks all have things that make them special. The zoo has animals and plants and sounds and smells from all over the world. An amusement park has rides and games and prizes and lots of cotton candy.

And all of these places have something in common. They all have a decorated entrance that tells you that you are about to enter a very different and exciting place.

Tonight, Jews all over the world are going to a magical place. The seder. A place filled with special foods, with family and friends and with exciting stories. And kiddush is the entrance into the seder.

When the person leading your seder stands up with a beautiful cup in his hand filled with wine and begins to say the kiddush, he is actually welcoming everyone to a very wonderful place. A place where you will hear stories from three thousand years ago. A place where frogs might jump on your table, where hail might fall from the ceiling and where you will get special treats, prizes and delicious foods.

URECHATZ (WASHING THE HANDS)

59
DSK

The procedure for washing one's hands is identical to when one washes before eating bread or matzah. Everyone except the leader of the seder should go to the kitchen. A large cup is filled with water. The water is poured twice on the right hand and twice on the left. Hands are dried, but no blessing is recited. Where possible; a cup, wash basin and towel should be brought to the table for the person leading the seder.

KARPAS (VEGETABLE)

Everyone should have a small piece of vegetable (celery or green pepper will suffice), that they will dip into salt–water. Before eating the vegetable a blessing is recited. This blessing not only relates to the karpas, but one should keep in mind that it also pertains to the maror, the bitter herbs, that will we be eaten later.

Blessed are You, Adonai, our God King of the universe, who creates the fruit of the ground.

בָּרוּךְ אַתָּה יְהֹוָה אֱלֹהֵינוּ מֶלֶךְ הָעוֹלָם, בּוֹרֵא פְּרִי הָאֲדָמָה:

Baruch attah Adonai, eloheynu melech ha-olam, boray p'ri ha-adamah.

YACHATZ (BREAK THE MATZAH)

63
DSK

The leader of the seder breaks the middle matzah in half. The smaller piece is put back between the two remaining whole matzahs. The larger half is wrapped up to be used later as the afikomen.

KARPAS

Imagine if your family didn't have a refrigerator. Milk would go sour very quickly, so you could only buy a little at a time. Often, instead of cereal and milk for breakfast, you would just have dry cereal instead. You probably like cold Coca-Cola or Hawaiian Punch or maybe lemonade in the summer. Well, without a refrigerator, you would almost never have anything cold to drink. A lot of things would be very different if you didn't have a refrigerator.

Now imagine if only a few families in your whole city had a refrigerator and yours was one of those families. Imagine how special it would feel every time you got to drink a cold glass of chocolate milk. If you lived in a city like that, then something as simple as drinking a cold coke would be looked at as a great privilege. A cold coke would be a very special treat; something people would look forward to, and something other people might never taste in their whole life.

Not too long ago there were no refrigerators. (Ask your grandparents if they had one when they were young). In the days before refrigerators it was considered special to have vegetables at a meal. Often, only very rich people had lots of vegetables. Sometimes only people like kings and their families got to eat lots of vegetables. In those days a vegetable appetizer was a sign of great wealth.

Karpas represents a vegetable appetizer that is a sign of wealth. On Passover every Jew is supposed to feel wealthy and special because being Jewish is something very, very special.

And do you know why we dip our karpas in salt water? Because the bitterness reminds us that at the same time that we feel wealthy, we also remember other people who aren't as fortunate as we are. Some people don't have food and some people don't have a seder, but tonight we are blessed with both.

YACHATZ

Imagine what it would be like if one night you asked your mother what she was making for lunch the next day and she told you that you were all out of food, that there was no money left to buy anything at the store and that you might have to ask some of your friends at school if they could share their lunch with you. How would you feel? What would you do?

When the Jewish people were slaves in Egypt they never knew if they would have food to eat from one day to the next. Sometimes they didn't even know if they would have food for their next meal. Often what they would do is eat less at one meal than they really wanted, and save the rest for the next meal in case they wouldn't have any other food.

When we break the matzah in half and put away a piece for later, it reminds us of the pain that families just like ours felt when they were slaves in Egypt.

This is a true story: A story about slavery, food, suffering and love.

Livia and her mother were prisoners at the German slave labor camp of Plaszow, located just outside of a large Polish city named Cracow. The work was very hard and they had little to eat. They were given stale bread, watery soup, an occasional onion or potato and very little else. At night they slept on wooden bunk beds and often three or four or even more girls had to share one bed. One night a bed collapsed from the weight of too many people. Twelve girls came crashing down on Livia's mother. Her back and neck were badly hurt and she could barely move.

In places like Plaszow when people were taken to the camp infirmary, if they didn't get better quickly they were usually killed. The doctors and nurses couldn't waste their time taking care of Jews who wouldn't be able to go back to work quickly. Livia went to see her mother every day. She did everything she could to help her mother regain her strength.

Eventually, Livia's mother regained enough strength to leave the infirmary. A while later they were shipped to Germany where they worked as slaves in a factory.

One day a group of girls that included Livia was told to go outside and shovel snow during a blizzard. They were all sure that they would die in the cold and they refused to listen. As a punishment, they were sent back to work in the factory and would be given no food for the next twenty-four hours. When Livia finally returned to the barracks her mother had a bowl of soup that she had saved for her. She had kept it warm under her blanket. But Livia, knowing how weak her mother was, refused to take the soup. Livia's mother looked at her young daughter and said, "I would rather spill this soup on the ground than eat it instead of my daughter who has worked for twenty-four hours without food." "I will not take it," was Livia's reply. Her mother spilled the soup on the ground. The two then looked at one another, embraced and cried the entire night.

Livia and her mother were amongst the few who were fortunate enough to survive their years in the slave labor and concentration camps. Of all that they suffered, the night of the spilled soup was their most painful.

MAGGID (THE HAGGADAH)

18
PSK

We are about to begin reading and discussing the main portion of the Haggadah text. Everyone present is invited to add their own thoughts and observations. The goal of this evening is to explore the origins of our people and the meaning of our Jewish identity as it is revealed through the Haggadah.

The leader of the seder now lifts the matzah for everyone to see and reads the following paragraph.

This is the simple, poor bread that our ancestors ate when they were slaves in the land of Egypt. But we are not poor, oppressed slaves anymore; we even have enough to invite others to join us at the seder. So we declare: Anyone who is hungry—is invited to eat with us. Anyone who needs a place—is invited to celebrate Passover with us. It's true, much has changed for the Jewish people, yet we continue to work for an even brighter future. Now we are here; next year may we be in the Land of Israel. Now we are slaves; next year may we be free.

הָא לַחְמָא עַנְיָא דִּי אֲכָלוּ אַבְהָתָנָא בְּאַרְעָא דְמִצְרָיִם. כָּל דִּכְפִין יֵיתֵי וְיֵיכוֹל, כָּל דִּצְרִיךְ יֵיתֵי וְיִפְסַח. הַשַּׁתָּא הָכָא, לְשָׁנָה הַבָּאָה בְּאַרְעָא דְיִשְׂרָאֵל. הַשַּׁתָּא עַבְדִּין לְשָׁנָה הַבָּאָה בְּנֵי חוֹרִין:

Anyone who needs a place is invited

Rebellious Child: Now we're inviting guests to the Seder! How insincere can you get? The Seder has already begun and there is no one around to invite!

Answer: Clearly the invitation to "anyone who needs a place" cannot be addressed to potential guests. Rather, we now lift our eyes from the Haggadah and address these words to those who are with us tonight. Sometimes, in our concern for people in far-off lands, we overlook the needs of those who are closest to us. At this point we reflect on our feelings for one another, for family, and for friends. It is time to let those who are right next to us know that their needs are important to us: That we are concerned, that we care, and that we will always be there for them.

This is a good time to think about what someone close to you needs, and how you can either assist or facilitate assistance. These needs can be physical, emotional, or spiritual.

When do we get to the ten plagues?

Simple Child: I'm hungry, do we have to read the whole Haggadah?

Answer: The reading of the Haggadah is far more than the telling of an overdone bedtime story. The reading of the Haggadah addresses itself to the innate human longing to know whence we came. Our present is profoundly linked to our past, and a murky notion of our origins will contribute to a sense of lonely detachment and inner estrangement. A child without a history is a child in search of place and purpose.

At the very least, and this is truly so very much, the Passover Seder confronts us with the responsibility of giving our children a sense of rootedness and belonging, of identity and direction. This Haggadah, we tell our children, this saga, is your saga. These events are your history, and these people are your people. Likewise, the ideas and values contained in the Haggadah are yours to consider. They are your inheritance, your family fortune.

The Haggadah tells us—as we tell our children—"You are a Jew." This is your past, your present, and the essence of your destiny.

Fun Facts Begin Here—Have Fun!   (Answers on pg. 97)
1) What does the word seder mean?
2) Why do we recline at the seder?
3) Which side should you recline on, and why?
4) Name the three patriarchs (founding fathers of the Jewish people).

Mahnishtana: The Four Questions

The Seder and the Haggadah both put special emphasis on encouraging the participation of children. For this reason it is customary for children to ask "The Four Questions."

The Seder plate is removed from in front of the leader of the seder, and the second of four cups of wine is poured. It is customary for people to pour wine for one another. The youngest child then asks the four questions.

Why is this night different from all other nights?

1. On all other nights we eat chometz (like cookies and crackers) or matzah, but on this night—only matzah.

2. On all other nights we eat all kinds of vegetables, but on this night—we make sure to eat bitter herbs.

3. On all other nights we do not have to dip our food even once, but on this night—we dip twice. First we dip our karpas in salt-water, and then we dip the bitter herbs in charoses.

4. On all other nights we eat either sitting or reclining, but on this night—we all recline.

מַה נִּשְׁתַּנָּה הַלַּיְלָה הַזֶּה מִכָּל הַלֵּילוֹת ?

שֶׁבְּכָל הַלֵּילוֹת אָנוּ אוֹכְלִין חָמֵץ אוֹ מַצָּה, הַלַּיְלָה הַזֶּה—כֻּלּוֹ מַצָּה:

שֶׁבְּכָל הַלֵּילוֹת אָנוּ אוֹכְלִין שְׁאָר יְרָקוֹת, הַלַּיְלָה הַזֶּה—מָרוֹר:

שֶׁבְּכָל הַלֵּילוֹת אֵין אָנוּ מַטְבִּילִין אֲפִילוּ פַּעַם אֶחָת, הַלַּיְלָה הַזֶּה—שְׁתֵּי פְעָמִים:

שֶׁבְּכָל הַלֵּילוֹת אָנוּ אוֹכְלִין בֵּין יוֹשְׁבִין וּבֵין מְסֻבִּין, הַלַּיְלָה הַזֶּה—כֻּלָּנוּ מְסֻבִּין:

MAHNISHTANA

You know, not all Jewish children get to go to a seder tonight. And that makes you very lucky.

Because Passover started a very long time ago, some families have forgotten that they are supposed to have a seder. The children in those families won't get to do all the things you will be doing.   They won't get matzah or charoses, they won't hear about the ten plagues and they won't get to look for the afikomen.

So after you have asked your parents the four questions, why don't you ask them one more question, a fifth question. **The Fifth Question:** "In many other families there is no seder, but in our family there still is. Please tell me—why did you decide that we should have a seder?"

MAHNISHTANA — WHY IS THIS NIGHT DIFFERENT...

The Mahnishtana is clearly calling our attention to a unique night. A nighttime, a period of darkness, unlike any other. And so we ask, why *is* this night different?

There is so much darkness in life. Dark cavernous voids that gnaw away at us. Darkness that clouds our vision of one another. Our ability to touch, to communicate, and to love. Darkness that pits us one against the other. Brother against brother, man against wife, nation against nation. And, in the dark of night, the Jewish nation was born. Surrounded by darkness while guided by the luminous rays of freedom.

Why is this night different? Because on this night we experienced our freedom. Why is this night different? Because only on this holiday do all the special observances, *mitzvot*, apply only at night. On Rosh Hashanah we blow the shofar only during the day. On Sukkot we sit in a sukkah during the day or night. Only on Passover do so many mitzvot apply only at night. Why is this night different? Why is this the only night of the year so brimming with mitzvot? Because on the night of Passover we not only commemorate the moment of our birth, but we express the very meaning of our existence as a people. Our sages tell us, *"For the mitzvah is like a candle and the Torah a light."*

The purpose of Jewish existence is to be a source of light where otherwise darkness would hold sway.

Mahnishtana: Why is this night different? Because dark as our lives may seem, lost though the world may have become, we still believe in the power of light. To illuminate our lives and our potential. To be a radiant force for all mankind. This is our message, and our mission. And we will not rest until the dark night again shines like the day.

---

5) Which one of the patriarchs lived in Egypt?
6) Why do we eat matzah on Passover?
7) What types of flour can matzah be made of?

The seder plate is brought back, the matzah remains uncovered and everyone reads and discusses the Haggadah.

85
PSK

Along, long time ago, we were slaves to Pharaoh in Egypt, but then God took us out from there. And when God rescued us from slavery it felt as if a mighty hand and an outstretched arm had reached out and saved us. Now let's imagine what it would be like if God would never have saved us from Egypt. In that case we, our children, and even our grandchildren would still be slaves to Pharaoh in Egypt. So even if we all know a lot about Jewish history, and even if we are all very wise, very understanding, and have lots of experience and knowledge of the Torah; there is still a mitzvah for us to tell about what happened when the Jews were saved from Egypt. You see, what happened in Egypt is not just history, it affected us too. The more one tells about leaving Egypt, the more we will all learn and the more praiseworthy it is.

עֲבָדִים הָיִינוּ לְפַרְעֹה בְּמִצְרָיִם, וַיּוֹצִיאֵנוּ יְהֹוָה אֱלֹהֵינוּ מִשָּׁם בְּיָד חֲזָקָה וּבִזְרֹעַ נְטוּיָה. וְאִלּוּ לֹא הוֹצִיא הַקָּדוֹשׁ בָּרוּךְ הוּא אֶת־אֲבוֹתֵינוּ מִמִּצְרָיִם, הֲרֵי אָנוּ וּבָנֵינוּ וּבְנֵי בָנֵינוּ מְשֻׁעְבָּדִים הָיִינוּ לְפַרְעֹה בְּמִצְרָיִם. וַאֲפִילוּ כֻּלָּנוּ חֲכָמִים, כֻּלָּנוּ נְבוֹנִים, כֻּלָּנוּ יוֹדְעִים אֶת־הַתּוֹרָה, מִצְוָה עָלֵינוּ לְסַפֵּר בִּיצִיאַת מִצְרָיִם. וְכָל הַמַּרְבֶּה לְסַפֵּר בִּיצִיאַת מִצְרַיִם, הֲרֵי זֶה מְשֻׁבָּח:

WE WERE SLAVES

When the Jewish people were slaves in Egypt they had to work very, very hard. Their job was to make bricks for the Egyptians to build their buildings with. The bricks were made out of straw and dirt and water, and every Jew had to make a certain amount of bricks every day. The Egyptian taskmasters were very mean and cruel. They were also always happy. If the Jews made enough bricks, they were happy. And if the Jews didn't make enough bricks they were also happy, because they got to beat the Jews who hadn't made enough bricks that day.

There was one Jew who was perfectly safe and who never had to be a slave. In fact, although he was a Jew, he was also an Egyptian prince. That prince's name was Moses.

This is the story of Moses.

Pharoah, the king of the Egyptians, ordered his officers to kill Jewish baby boys. He was afraid that one of these boys might grow-up to save the Jews, so he wanted to protect himself by killing the baby boys. When Mose's mother, Yocheved, gave birth she was afraid that her baby would be killed. In an attempt to save her baby, she made a special basket for him and then left the basket in some tall grass at the edge of the Nile river. She prayed that an Egyptian woman would have mercy on her baby, and she sent her daughter, Miriam, to watch what happened.

Something wonderful happened. An Egyptian woman named Basya found the baby and decided to raise him as her own child. Basya was a very special person, not only because of the mercy she showed a Jewish baby, but because she was the daughter of Pharoah himself. But there was a problem. Little baby Moses wouldn't eat and Basya was very upset. Fortunately, Miriam was able to help Basya and she offered to bring a woman to nurse the baby. And guess who that woman was? It was the baby's very own mother, Yocheved. So Moses was raised as a prince in the palace of Pharoah, but because his nurse was also his real mother, Moses learned that he was really a Jew.

One day when Moses was already a young prince, he saw an Egyptian taskmaster cruelly beating a Jewish slave. Though he owed his life to the Egyptians who saved him as a baby, Moses could not stand by and watch a fellow Jew be beaten. Moses killed the taskmaster. Because of this, Moses had to run away from Egypt because if he was caught, Pharoah would have him put to death for killing the Egyptian.

Moses was willing to give up his luxurious life as an Egyptian prince and risk his life to protect another Jew. This is why God chose Moses to lead the Jewish people out of Egypt.

...if G-d would never have saved us from Egypt

Wise Child: With all that has transpired in the world over the last 3,000 years, is it really conceivable that if G-d had not taken us out of Egypt that we would still be there today?

Answer: The enslavement mentioned in this section is an allusion to the multilayered meaning of slavery. And, just as slavery has connotations beyond physical bondage, so the reference to Egypt is more than just a geographic location.

While we would all like to think of ourselves as being perfect, fortunately, life often reminds us that we are not. As a result, when our car breaks down we call a mechanic, when our tooth hurts we visit the dentist, and when life aches we seek out one of the practitioners of therapy or recovery with which our society is teeming. We all know that there are times when we need resources outside of ourselves who can assist us in identifying or solving a problem, charting a course, or achieving a goal.

The Hebrew word for Egypt, *Mitzrayim*, means *constrain* or *stifle*. A slave is certainly constrained and stifled. And aren't we all? Can't we all admit to ourselves that there are aspects of our lives that seem to be beyond our control—or anyone else's? That no matter how desperately we want something, we can't seem to discipline ourselves in ways that will facilitate achievement? That no matter how hard we try, we keep making the same mistakes over and over again? Well, how about this for a radical idea—ask G-d for help! It's not like He took early retirement after the exodus from Egypt, you know.

If the proverbial atheist in a foxhole will always turn to God for help, why can't we? Perhaps you could say that another way to translate Mitzrayim—is foxhole, and as we know, life is full of little foxholes.

Note: *When you go to a mechanic or doctor you are hardly "copping out." On the contrary, you are being mature, intelligent, and resourceful. Likewise with God. Judaism never advocates the abdication of responsibility to G-d, rather it submits that in our earnest efforts to achieve what we want, we often need help—even God's.*

---

8) What does the word Haggadah mean?
9) Which of Jacob's sons was the first to live in Egypt?
10) How did Joseph get to Egypt?
11) Name the four matriarchs (founding mothers of the Jewish people).
12) How many plagues happened to the Egyptians?

Some people feel that the seder is longer than it needs to be. I hope that tonight you're not one of those people and that your seder is enjoyable and insightful. However, if you are getting a little edgy–well–read on and be glad that you're not in Bnei Brak.

In ancient Israel there were many great and wise Torah scholars. Once, during the time of the second Temple (about 1900 years ago), five of the most prominent scholars; Rabbi Eliezer, Rabbi Yehoshua, Rabbi Elazar ben Azaryah, Rabbi Akiva, and Rabbi Tarfon were all having a Seder together in the city of Bnei Brak. Each of them was a wise sage who knew a great deal about what happened in Egypt, but nonetheless, they spent the entire night discussing the miracles that took place when the Jews were saved. As a matter of fact, they never even went to sleep and their discussion continued until their students came to tell them that it was time for the morning prayer services.

You have probably heard about the Talmud, though it's quite likely you never had a chance to study it. Tonight you will have that opportunity because the Haggadah contains some brief excerpts from the Talmud.

The Talmud is a huge collection of volumes that span thousands of pages and contains hundreds of discussions by great sages on every aspect of Jewish law and life. A frequent topic in the Talmud is the discussion and debate about the application of various aspects of halachah (Jewish Law). Another topic the sages address is the identification of precise verses in the Torah that serve as the basis for a particular halachah (law).

The Haggadah contains a few examples of Talmudic discussions that relate to Passover and the rescue of the Jewish people from Egypt. The upcoming paragraph in the Haggadah is an example of a discussion about identifying a source in the Torah for a particular halachah.

Some people refer to the Talmud as a sea, because it is so vast. So get ready– we're about to jump into the great sea of Talmudic learning.

According to halacha (Jewish law), there is an obligation to mention the Exodus from Egypt every day during the morning and evening prayer service. The question is: Where in the Torah do we find mention of such an obligation? Let's listen in on a Talmudic discussion that took place around two thousand years ago.

Rabbi Elazar ben Azaryah knew the source in the Torah for the obligation to mention the Exodus during the morning

89/90
DSK

services, but he wasn't sure which verse actually indicated that there is a similar obligation in the evening. In regard to this matter, Rabbi Elazar ben Azaryah once said: "I was like a seventy year old man, but I still could not pinpoint a source in the Torah that relates to mentioning the Exodus from Egypt even at night. Then my colleague, Ben Zoma, expounded upon the verse which says: *'In order that you may remember the day you left Egypt all the days of your life'*. Ben Zoma taught me that the words *'the days of your life,'* are referring specifically to the daytime. This means that every day we must remember the Exodus, and the way we do this is by mentioning it in our daily prayers. Then he went on to teach me that the addition of the word *'all,'* means that at all times of the day—even at night—you must remember the Exodus. Thanks to Ben Zoma, I now know which verse in the Torah instructs us to mention the Exodus during both the morning and evening prayer service. However, there were other sages that disagreed with Ben Zoma. They taught that *'the days of your life,'* refers only to the world as we now know it; the addition of the word *'all'* means that we must continue to remember the Exodus even after the arrival of the Messiah.

I can't wait 'till we get to the ten plagues.

מַעֲשֶׂה בְּרַבִּי אֱלִיעֶזֶר וְרַבִּי יְהוֹשֻׁעַ וְרַבִּי אֶלְעָזָר בֶּן עֲזַרְיָה וְרַבִּי עֲקִיבָא וְרַבִּי טַרְפוֹן שֶׁהָיוּ מְסֻבִּין בִּבְנֵי בְרַק. וְהָיוּ מְסַפְּרִים בִּיצִיאַת מִצְרַיִם כָּל אוֹתוֹ הַלַּיְלָה עַד שֶׁבָּאוּ תַלְמִידֵיהֶם וְאָמְרוּ לָהֶם, רַבּוֹתֵינוּ הִגִּיעַ זְמַן קְרִיאַת שְׁמַע שֶׁל שַׁחֲרִית:

אָמַר רַבִּי אֶלְעָזָר בֶּן עֲזַרְיָה הֲרֵי אֲנִי כְּבֶן שִׁבְעִים שָׁנָה, וְלֹא זָכִיתִי שֶׁתֵּאָמֵר יְצִיאַת מִצְרַיִם בַּלֵּילוֹת עַד שֶׁדְּרָשָׁהּ בֶּן זוֹמָא. שֶׁנֶּאֱמַר, לְמַעַן תִּזְכֹּר אֶת־יוֹם צֵאתְךָ מֵאֶרֶץ מִצְרַיִם כֹּל יְמֵי חַיֶּיךָ. יְמֵי חַיֶּיךָ הַיָּמִים. כֹּל יְמֵי חַיֶּיךָ לְהָבִיא הַלֵּילוֹת. וַחֲכָמִים אוֹמְרִים, יְמֵי חַיֶּיךָ הָעוֹלָם הַזֶּה. כֹּל יְמֵי חַיֶּיךָ לְהָבִיא לִימוֹת הַמָּשִׁיחַ:

All the days of your life

Rebellious Child: Isn't this a bit obsessive? All day, all night, my whole life! Isn't it enough to remember the exodus on Passover and that will cover you for the year?

Answer: Remember the first baseball game your father took you to? The first time you told your husband you loved him; the birth of your first child or your first date? There is something magical about first times in life. The impression they make on our souls is indelible, their resonant feelings are ever present.

Years later, when we find ourselves in need of inspiration, we can journey back to those magical firsts. Once again we can access that inventive state of mind, burst of creativity, or impulse to greatness. It is this journey in search of renewed inspiration to which Ben Zoma is directing us. Everyday, when Jews recite the *Shema* and recall the exodus from Egypt, they attempt to return to that seminal moment of liberation. In so doing they strive to keep their commitments as vital and animate as the day they were born.

Blessed is the Place. Blessed is God who is everywhere, blessed is He. Blessed is the One Who gave the Torah to His nation, the people of Israel; blessed is He. When studying the Torah we find that there are four kinds of children and that each one needs to be taught about Passover in a different way: There is one child who knows all about being Jewish and is wise, another one who also knows a lot about Judaism, but is rebellious; one who is simple, and one who never had a chance to learn and who doesn't even know what to ask.

בָּרוּךְ הַמָּקוֹם, בָּרוּךְ הוּא. בָּרוּךְ שֶׁנָּתַן תּוֹרָה לְעַמּוֹ יִשְׂרָאֵל, בָּרוּךְ הוּא. כְּנֶגֶד אַרְבָּעָה בָנִים דִּבְּרָה תוֹרָה. אֶחָד חָכָם, וְאֶחָד רָשָׁע, וְאֶחָד תָּם, וְאֶחָד שֶׁאֵינוֹ יוֹדֵעַ לִשְׁאוֹל:

---

13) What are the names of the five books of the Torah?

14) What is the main topic of each of the five books?

15) How many books are there in the Torah?

16) How many mitzvot (commandments) are there in the Torah?

17) Passover is one of the "three festivals" (shalosh regalim), what are the other two?

18) What happened to Joseph in Egypt?

19) What part of Egypt did the Jewish people live in?

BLESSED IS THE PLACE

Physicists and cosmologists like Stephen W. Hawking tell us that at the moment of the big bang the "size" of the universe was zero, and that "before" the Big Bang there was no time, space, matter or energy. To figure out this puzzle, all you have to do is close your eyes and see what appears when you eliminate time, space, matter and energy from your mind's eye. Go ahead—give it a try. If you are having a hard time, that's okay, because even if all you saw was darkness, it had to be a darkness that filled a space, and remember—there was no space!

Are you scratching your head, wondering where the universe came from? Well, the Haggadah has an answer to this puzzle. The Haggadah calls it *Hamakom*. The primordial Place.

The previous paragraph in the Haggadah told us that the Torah refers to four different children. The section we are about to read deals specifically with those children.

The holiday of Passover not only celebrates our liberation from slavery, but it also marks the birth of the Jewish people. When we first went to Egypt we were just a family–the family of Jacob and his children–but when we left we became *Am Yisroel*, the nation of Israel.

The seder commemorates the birth of our people and the context of the seder is a dialogue between parents and children. There is no better time than tonight for parents to think about what makes each of their children unique and special, and there is no better time to think about what you want to tell your children about the meaning of being a Jew. Our ability to communicate with our children is the cornerstone of the Jewish people.

94-105
פסח

The wise child–what does he say? 'I would like to know everything about the laws, statutes and ordinances that God, has commanded you to do?' Since this child is very motivated to learn, you should explain to him all the laws of the Passover. You should be very careful not to leave anything out and even teach him the very last detail of the Passover laws: namely, that nothing may be eaten after the afikomen–the final taste of the Passover meal.

The rebellious child–what does he say? 'Why do you bother with all these laws?' He looks at the laws of Passover and says that they are for you. By saying 'you', he is implying that he

doesn't want to be a part of the rest of us. He doesn't really care if he is a part of the Jewish people or not. And since he excludes himself from the Jewish people, this means he is denying God, the basic principle of Judaism. Therefore, you need to give him a very tough answer and tell him: 'It is because of these very laws that God did miracles for me when I went out of Egypt.' The Torah says, 'For me,' but not for people like him—because had he been there, he would not have been saved.

The simple child—what does he say? 'What is this?' To this child you must carefully and gently explain to him: 'The reason we celebrate Passover and are careful about all these laws is because God used His mighty hand to rescue our ancestors from slavery in Egypt.

As for the child who doesn't know what to ask— you need to help him get started. As it says in the Torah, 'You shall tell your child on the day of Passover: It is because of these laws of Passover that God did miracles for me when I went out of Egypt.'

חָכָם מַה הוּא אוֹמֵר? מָה הָעֵדֹת וְהַחֻקִּים וְהַמִּשְׁפָּטִים אֲשֶׁר צִוָּה יְהוָה אֱלֹהֵינוּ אֶתְכֶם? וְאַף אַתָּה אֱמֹר לוֹ כְּהִלְכוֹת הַפֶּסַח, אֵין מַפְטִירִין אַחַר הַפֶּסַח אֲפִיקוֹמָן:

רָשָׁע מַה הוּא אוֹמֵר? מָה הָעֲבוֹדָה הַזֹּאת לָכֶם? לָכֶם וְלֹא לוֹ. וּלְפִי שֶׁהוֹצִיא אֶת־עַצְמוֹ מִן הַכְּלָל, כָּפַר בְּעִקָּר. וְאַף אַתָּה הַקְהֵה אֶת־שִׁנָּיו. וֶאֱמָר לוֹ, בַּעֲבוּר זֶה עָשָׂה יְהוָה לִי בְּצֵאתִי מִמִּצְרָיִם. לִי וְלֹא לוֹ, אִלּוּ הָיָה שָׁם לֹא הָיָה נִגְאָל:

תָּם מַה הוּא אוֹמֵר? מַה זֹּאת? וְאָמַרְתָּ אֵלָיו, בְּחֹזֶק יָד הוֹצִיאָנוּ יְהוָה מִמִּצְרַיִם מִבֵּית עֲבָדִים:

וְשֶׁאֵינוֹ יוֹדֵעַ לִשְׁאוֹל, אַתְּ פְּתַח לוֹ שֶׁנֶּאֱמַר, וְהִגַּדְתָּ לְבִנְךָ בַּיּוֹם הַהוּא לֵאמֹר, בַּעֲבוּר זֶה עָשָׂה יְהוָה לִי בְּצֵאתִי מִמִּצְרָיִם:

20) What are the five mitzvot (commandments) unique to the seder?
21) What happened seven days after the Jewish people left Egypt?
22) What happened on Mt. Sinai?

You shall tell your child

Simple Child: I don't get it—is the Torah only for children?

Answer: The Torah is for everyone. Young or old, good or bad, educated or not. You see, to the Almighty, we are all children. In no other endeavor is the playing field so level, the rules so meritocratic, than in the human quest for a relationship with God. It doesn't matter what your profession is, where you've been, or what you have or haven't done in life. Like a loving parent, God is always there. The path to spiritual closeness to God is open to us all.

Nothing may be eaten after the afikomen

Wise Child: If you are supposed to teach the wise son all the laws of Passover, then why single out the laws of afikomen for specific mention?

Answer: Would Disney World be worth the trip if you had to come home empty-handed? No video, no photos, not even a postcard or T-shirt of Mickey? Perhaps in our rush to preserve every experience we have on some form of tape or film, we are in fact sacrificing a great deal. As we assume our position behind the camera and begin to stalk the big game of "Kodak moments," are we not also removing ourselves from the picture? Do we not become detached observers as well as active participants?

The law of the afikomen—namely, that once it's over—it's over, is a hint at the lost spiritual art of savoring. The art of savoring is a sensitization technique that allows us to become completely immersed in an experience. In Judaism this discipline of savoring, of emotional and intellectual relish, is essential to the path of personal growth known as Mussar.

The Jewish art of savoring bids us to fine-tune our senses and to become more fully absorbed in both vision, sound, and their attendant

23) What holiday celebrates the giving of the Torah?
24) Why do we drink four cups of wine at the seder?
25) How long were the Jews enslaved in Egypt?

feelings. In thought and ideas, as well as in internal impulses and their sources. To experience the dancing and the joy. The music, the tears, the love and the rarefied closeness they stir within us. To consciously engage every day and every moment; to celebrate life, and to imbibe the totality of every experiential step we take.

Upon concluding the Seder, Jewish law bids us not to taste anything after the afikomen. This is a night for savoring: Ideas, inspiration, and images. Parents teaching, children learning, and all of us growing together. Allow the experience to become a part of you. Savor this night of freedom. Only then can you leave. Not with souvenirs, not with photos, but as a different person. A different Jew. And this you will never forget.

Choose one moment you want to remember from the Seder—close your eyes, and savor it.

The laws, statutes and ordinances

Rebellious Child: If this kid is so wise, how come he doesn't seem to know very much about all this stuff?

Answer: Passover is known as *the time of our freedom*, and the wise son understands that the experience of the Seder is a precious opportunity which comes only once a year.

Inside each and every one of us lives a child of wisdom. We sense that there is more to Judaism than meets the eye. That what distinguishes a statute from an ordinance is more than just Jewish legal jargon, but rather a deeper set of ideas and spiritual concepts. That what separates one holiday from the next is not just the taste of seasonal delicacies, but distinctive opportunities for expanded consciousness. That under the rubric of Judaism is to be found something not only profound and insightful but deeply personal and enlightening.

Inside us all there is a voice that wants the privilege of a fully panoramic view of Judaism. To comprehend each facet of the Seder and how every nuance relates to the message of freedom, and the meaning of being a Jew. Listen to that voice. Refuse to sit there and just go through the motions. Be wise! Think, inquire and ask questions. Of Passover and its meaning for starters, and of Judaism and what it says about life as an encore.

Give him a very tough answer

Simple Child: Why are you so mad at him? At least he's here—cousin Mitchell didn't even come.

Answer: Don't mistake our harshness for anger. We love this child as much as we love you and every one else at the Seder tonight. If we didn't care deeply about him, we would have told him to take his cynicism and go somewhere else for Passover—but we didn't. Intent as he may be on hurtling himself into the oblivion of a pseudo identity, we will always remain eager to teach him. Along the way we may have to say a few things that are painful for him as well as for us; but sometimes there is no choice.

No, we're not mad, but when it comes to cousin Mitchell—indeed—we are very, very sad.

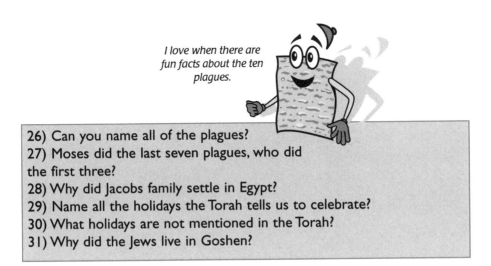

I love when there are fun facts about the ten plagues.

26) Can you name all of the plagues?
27) Moses did the last seven plagues, who did the first three?
28) Why did Jacobs family settle in Egypt?
29) Name all the holidays the Torah tells us to celebrate?
30) What holidays are not mentioned in the Torah?
31) Why did the Jews live in Goshen?

This next paragraph is another example of a Talmudic discussion related to Passover. To understand the context of this discussion you need to know that the Passover seder is celebrated on the 15th day of the Hebrew month of Nisan.

On the first day of Nisan, just two weeks before the Jews were rescued from Egypt, God instructed Moses to teach the Jews about the Passover Offering. In a sense, the process of redemption began on the first of Nisan. For this reason, you might think that the mitzvah to tell the story about leaving Egypt should also begin on the first day of Nisan, but the Torah says: *'You shall tell your child on that day.'* The expression *'on that day,'* could possibly mean only during the daytime. Therefore, to avoid any confusion, the Torah adds: *'It is because of this that God did wonders for me when I went out of Egypt.'* The word "this," implies the presence of something tangible, thus, *'You shall tell your child'* applies only when tangible items like matzah and maror are right in front of you. And when is this? Only on the night of the seder. Thus, though the process of redemption began on the first of Nisan, the mitzvah to tell the story does not apply until the fifteenth of Nisan at the seder.

יָכוֹל מֵרֹאשׁ חֹדֶשׁ, תַּלְמוּד לוֹמַר בַּיּוֹם הַהוּא. אִי בַּיּוֹם הַהוּא, יָכוֹל מִבְּעוֹד יוֹם, תַּלְמוּד לוֹמַר בַּעֲבוּר זֶה. בַּעֲבוּר זֶה לֹא אָמַרְתִּי אֶלָּא בְּשָׁעָה שֶׁיֵּשׁ מַצָּה וּמָרוֹר מֻנָּחִים לְפָנֶיךָ:

WHEN MATZAH AND MAROR ARE RIGHT IN FRONT OF YOU

Matzah represents freedom and is contrasted with maror, which represents the bitterness of slavery. If the Haggadah may be appropriately subtitled *The Book of Freedom*, then the question being probed here is this: When is the best time for someone to learn about freedom? And to this query the reply comes: "When matzah [freedom] and maror [slavery] are *right in front of you.*"

• Work has been one frustration after another, and now your daughter wants you to teach her how to hit a softball.
• Your friends have an extra ticket to a concert, but you need the time to study.

- Someone just took your parking spot.
- Your husband looks like he's had a rough day, though you are convinced yours has been even rougher.

Life is an ongoing process of dealing with choices. Being cognizant of our choices—of our capacity to control and direct our thoughts, words, actions, and reactions—is a prerequisite to freedom. These choices, some of them "big" but most of them not, are an ever-present reality. At all times they are quite literally *right in front of us*, and on some level each constitutes the choice between slavery and freedom.

This paragraph takes us all the way back to the very origins of the Jewish people. In the Torah, the story of the Jewish people begins with the life of Abraham. Abraham and Sarah and their son Isaac were the very first Jewish family. They lived in the Middle East around 3,500 years ago. This was approximately four hundred years before their descendants, the Jewish people, were freed from slavery in Egypt.

In those days everyone in the world prayed to idols, and even our ancestors were idol worshippers. Now, however, God has brought us close to Him. We know that you can have a relationship with the One real God. Regarding the earliest days of our people it says, "And Joshua (the leader of the Jewish people after the death of Moses) told the people, 'The God of Israel said; your ancestors lived on the other side of the river: Terach was the father of Avraham (Abraham) and Nachor, and they all served other gods. And then I took your father Avraham from the other side of the river and brought him to the land of Israel. I gave him many children and grandchildren. Avraham and Sarah's first son was Isaac. To Isaac I gave two sons, Jacob and Esau. To Esau I gave Mount Seir as a place to live, but Jacob and his children had to go down to Egypt.'**

מִתְּחִלָּה עוֹבְדֵי עֲבוֹדָה זָרָה הָיוּ אֲבוֹתֵינוּ, וְעַכְשָׁו קֵרְבָנוּ הַמָּקוֹם לַעֲבֹדָתוֹ.
שֶׁנֶּאֱמַר, וַיֹּאמֶר יְהוֹשֻׁעַ אֶל־כָּל־הָעָם, כֹּה־אָמַר יְהוָה אֱלֹהֵי יִשְׂרָאֵל בְּעֵבֶר הַנָּהָר
יָשְׁבוּ אֲבוֹתֵיכֶם מֵעוֹלָם, תֶּרַח אֲבִי אַבְרָהָם וַאֲבִי נָחוֹר, וַיַּעַבְדוּ אֱלֹהִים אֲחֵרִים:
וָאֶקַּח אֶת־אֲבִיכֶם אֶת־אַבְרָהָם מֵעֵבֶר הַנָּהָר וָאוֹלֵךְ אוֹתוֹ בְּכָל־אֶרֶץ כְּנָעַן,
וָאַרְבֶּה אֶת־זַרְעוֹ וָאֶתֶּן לוֹ אֶת־יִצְחָק: וָאֶתֵּן לְיִצְחָק אֶת־יַעֲקֹב וְאֶת־עֵשָׂו, וָאֶתֵּן
לְעֵשָׂו אֶת־הַר שֵׂעִיר לָרֶשֶׁת אוֹתוֹ, וְיַעֲקֹב וּבָנָיו יָרְדוּ מִצְרָיִם:

EVEN OUR ANCESTORS WERE IDOL WORSHIPPERS

Today when people pray, they pray to God. But that's not how it always was. People used to pray to things like the wind or the stars or even statues that they made out of wood or stone. These statues were called idols.

Abraham was the very first Jew, and when he was a young boy growing-up, nobody believed in God. As a matter of fact, Abraham's father's business was to make idols that other people could buy and pray to. Abraham was taught that there were many, many gods. But Abraham didn't believe that an idol could really be powerful. He didn't even believe that the mighty thunder, the deep oceans or even the big, bright sun should be prayed to.

One day Terach, Abraham's father, asked Abraham to take care of the family idol store while he was away. After Terach left, Abraham went into the room where all the idols were stored. Abraham picked up one of his father's hammers and began to smash all the idols. Pieces of idol went flying everywhere. (Imagine what would happen if you did that in your father's business.)

Abraham broke all of the idols except for the biggest one. He put the hammer into the hand of the biggest idol in the store, and then walked out leaving behind a terrible mess.

When Terach returned and saw what happened he was furious. "What happened," he demanded of his son. "I left you in charge and look what you did." Abraham told his father that he could explain everything. "You see," he said, "I left the store for twenty minutes, and while I was gone the biggest idol took one of your hammers and smashed all the other idols." "Look," Abraham said pointing to the biggest idol, "he still has the hammer in his hand." "Now Abraham," said Terach, "you know that an idol can't pick up a hammer." "Well father," asked Abraham, "If an idol can't even pick up a hammer, then why should anyone ever pray to an idol?"

From then on Abraham tried to teach anyone he could not to pray to idols, to the wind or to anything else they thought had special powers. "Pray to God, not idols," said Abraham, "God created the wind and the sun and everything else. God is the source of all power, God is One, and that's who we should all pray to."

FROM THE OTHER SIDE OF THE RIVER

Rachel's friend Chris had a really cool father. He worked as a DJ at WRCK and always got great concert tickets for Chris and his friends. Shelley was someone else with a really cool parent. Her mom managed a Mexican restaurant, and when Shelley came with her friends to eat there on Saturday nights her mom always let the waiter serve them a beer or two. Rachel loved the weekends with her friends, but she sensed that something bothered her parents. Rachel didn't feel totally comfortable with everything her friends did. They all smoked, they did other stuff too, but what could Rachel do? They were her friends.

"Rachel," said her very uncool father one Friday night before she went out with Shelley, "I want to tell you something." "Sure dad."

"When I was seventeen, some friends and I decided to break into our high school and steal the answers to a bunch of tests. We were going to use them for ourselves and maybe sell them to some other kids. When it came time to go through with it, I told my friends that I wasn't going. 'What are you, a chicken,' they said. To this day I don't know what came over me, but I told them that I was actually braver then any of them ever would be. And then I left; and so did they. I wish I could tell you that they got caught, but they didn't. As a matter of fact, they all did better than I did on most of those tests. But you know what? It didn't bother me one bit. I want you to know something Rachel." 'What is it dad?' "I trust you Rachel. I trust you a lot."

One of the toughest things in life is to be different from other people. Abraham, the first Jew, was different from everyone around him. That is what the Haggadah means when it says that Abraham came from the other side of the river. Inside each and every Jew is a soft voice that says, "I trust you."

Ask your parents if they ever had to be different from everyone else around them. Ask them why they did it and how it felt. You can also ask them if being Jewish ever made them feel different or uncomfortable. Ask them what happened and how they reacted.

Blessed is the One Who keeps His promise to the Jewish people; blessed is He. God calculated the right time to rescue us from slavery in Egypt. About two hundred and fifty years before the Jews became slaves in Egypt, God made an eternal covenant with Abraham and told him: 'You need to know that your children will be strangers in a foreign land. The people of that land will force your children into slavery and will brutally oppress them for four hundred years; but at the right time I will bring judgment on that nation, and afterwards your children will leave with great wealth'.

בָּרוּךְ שׁוֹמֵר הַבְטָחָתוֹ לְיִשְׂרָאֵל. בָּרוּךְ הוּא. שֶׁהַקָּדוֹשׁ בָּרוּךְ הוּא חִשֵּׁב אֶת־ הַקֵּץ לַעֲשׂוֹת כְּמָה שֶׁאָמַר לְאַבְרָהָם אָבִינוּ בִּבְרִית בֵּין הַבְּתָרִים. שֶׁנֶּאֱמַר, וַיֹּאמֶר לְאַבְרָם, יָדֹעַ תֵּדַע כִּי גֵר יִהְיֶה זַרְעֲךָ בְּאֶרֶץ לֹא לָהֶם, וַעֲבָדוּם וְעִנּוּ אֹתָם אַרְבַּע מֵאוֹת שָׁנָה: וְגַם אֶת־הַגּוֹי אֲשֶׁר יַעֲבֹדוּ דָּן אָנֹכִי, וְאַחֲרֵי כֵן יֵצְאוּ בִּרְכֻשׁ גָּדוֹל:

And will brutally oppress them for four hundred years

Wise Child: If you calculate the number of years from the arrival of Jacob and his family in Egypt (2238BCE), until redemption (2448BCE), you come up with a total of 210 years—what happened to the other 190 years?

Answer: The Hebrew word for Egypt, *Mitzrayim*, means to be trapped, stifled or smothered. Our mystical tradition tells us that those missing 190 years would eventually play themselves out during the future years of Jewish history and exile. The stifling presence of Egypt would be a nagging spiritual force that would hound the Jewish soul wherever it went. It was as if those one hundred and ninety years were ground into tiny specks of timedust, metaphysical milliseconds, if you will. Then, scattered across the eons, these smothering particles of Egypt work insidiously to suppress our ability—as individuals and as a nation—to scale the heights of spiritual potential.

But fear not. For just as the corporate glass ceiling can be pierced, so too this pernicious spiritual foe. Tonight, the Seder night, is known as *layl shimurim*, a night of shielding and security. The Seder is a spiritual refuge. A brief quietus during which the dust of Egypt is laid to rest. On this night of liberation we can see our struggles in a clearer light. We not only see where we have been stifled, but can also detect a way out. Tonight, each Jew, and thus the collective soul of the Jewish nation, can eclipse that which dares to constrain us and begin to move on to new vistas of freedom.

The matzah is covered and everyone lifts their cup of wine or grape juice. Together, everyone reads the following paragraph with a feeling of joy. Upon its conclusion, the cups are put down and the matzah is uncovered.

114-15
PSK

And it is that original promise of redemption that God made to Abraham that has sustained our forefathers as well as us. Because over the years more than one nation has attempted to destroy us. In fact, in each and every generation they try to destroy us, but God rescues us from their grasp.

וְהִיא שֶׁעָמְדָה לַאֲבוֹתֵינוּ וְלָנוּ, שֶׁלֹּא אֶחָד בִּלְבַד עָמַד עָלֵינוּ לְכַלּוֹתֵנוּ, אֶלָּא שֶׁבְּכָל־דּוֹר וָדוֹר עוֹמְדִים עָלֵינוּ לְכַלּוֹתֵנוּ, וְהַקָּדוֹשׁ בָּרוּךְ הוּא מַצִּילֵנוּ מִיָּדָם:

"...in each and every generation..."

Simple Child: Have non-Jews really tried to destroy us in every generation?

Answer: Consider the following…

---

32) Why do we have three matzahs at the seder?
33) Why do we have charoset at the seder?
34) If there are no children at the seder to tell the story to, do you still have to read the Haggadah?

1430BCE — Slavery in Egypt.

356BCE — Achashverosh, King of Persia, decrees death
to all his Jewish subjects.

138BCE — Syrian-Greek government outlaws the practice of
Judaism in Israel.

400CE — Saint John Chrysostom calls Jews "lustful, rapa-
cious, greedy, perfidious bandits; inveterate
murderers."

486 — Monks and mobs burn synagogue, dig up a Jewish
cemetery, and burn bones.

624 — Mohammed watches as 600 Jews are decapitated
in Medina in one day.

640 — Jews expelled from Arabia.

1096 — First crusade: Thousands of Jews tortured and
massacred.

1146 — Second crusade: Thousands of Jews, including women
and babies, are butchered across Europe.

1200s — Jews "cause" the Black Plague. Jews murdered in
Frankfort, Speyer, Koblenz, Mainz, Cracow, Alsace,
Bonn, and other cities.

1290 — Jews expelled from England.

1306 — First expulsion of Jews from France.

1349 — Jews expelled from Hungary.

1391 — Spain: Seville, Majorca, Barcelona—tens of thousands
of Jews killed.

1394 — Second expulsion from France.

1400's — Jews accused of murdering Christian children and
baking matzah with the blood.

1421 — Jews expelled from Austria

1492 — Jews expelled from Spain.

1496 — Jews expelled from Portugal

1500–1600s — The bones of Gracia de Orta, a Jewish scientist
and "convert" to Christianity, are exhumed and burnt

because he was a Marrano (secret Jew). Elsewhere, Marranos are burned in Mexico, Portugal, Peru, and Spain.

1553 —The Talmud is burned in public bonfires in Italy.

1648–66 —Cossacks, Poles, Russians, and Swedes massacre Jews.

1744 —Jews expelled from Bohemia and Moravia.

1818 —Pogroms in Yemen.

1840 —Blood libel in Damascus.

1862 —General Ulysses S. Grant expels Jews from Tennessee.

1882 —Pogroms in Russia.

1930s–40s—Official Canadian reply to most Jewish pleas for refuge: "Unfortunately, though we greatly sympathize with your circumstance, at present you cannot be admitted. Please try some other country." (Of course, there were no other countries; only the gates of Auschwitz remained open.)

1939–45 —Six million Jews are annihilated across Europe. Babies serve as target practice, women are human guinea pigs for doctors and scientists, beards are torn from men's faces.

1948–67 —Fearing for their lives; Jews flee Algeria, Iraq, Syria, Yemen and Egypt.

1917–91 —The study of Hebrew is a "crime against the state" in the former Soviet Union.

1992–94 —The Committee for Open Debate on the Holocaust runs full-page ads in university newspapers across the U.S. claiming that the Holocaust never took place.

1993 —Anti-Jewish publications sell briskly in Japan. A leading Japanese newspaper carries an ad that reveals a Jewish plot to weaken and enslave Japan.

If we want to see how God saves us from our enemies, let's begin by looking at a story in the Torah: The story of Jacob and Esau.

Due to a conflict with his brother Esau, Jacob had to flee from his parents home and go live with his uncle Laban. At first Laban seemed to be warm and welcoming, but before long he showed his true, treacherous colors.

Let's go learn what Laban the Aramean tried to do to our **father Jacob. We know that Pharaoh was a terrible enemy of the Jewish people, but he only decreed that baby boys should be killed. Laban, on the other hand, wanted to destroy Jacob's entire family.**

This is what it says in the Torah; "Laban the Aramean tried to totally destroy my father, Jacob. Then, after surviving Laban's plans for destruction, Jacob and his small family descended to Egypt and sojourned there; and there he became a nation— great, powerful, and numerous."

Now we are going to study the verse from the Torah that talks about Jacob's descent to Egypt and see what we can learn. The highlighted text is a quote from the Torah and is followed by an insight.

Jacob and his small family descended to Egypt— this **means that Jacob would have rather stayed in Israel, but God created circumstances that forced him to go down to Egypt.**

צֵא וּלְמַד מַה־בִּקֵּשׁ לָבָן הָאֲרַמִּי לַעֲשׂוֹת לְיַעֲקֹב אָבִינוּ. שֶׁפַּרְעֹה לֹא גָזַר אֶלָּא עַל הַזְּכָרִים, וְלָבָן בִּקֵּשׁ לַעֲקוֹר אֶת־הַכֹּל. שֶׁנֶּאֱמַר, אֲרַמִּי אֹבֵד אָבִי, וַיֵּרֶד מִצְרַיְמָה וַיָּגָר שָׁם בִּמְתֵי מְעָט, וַיְהִי שָׁם לְגוֹי גָּדוֹל, עָצוּם וָרָב:

וַיֵּרֶד מִצְרַיְמָה—אָנוּס עַל פִּי הַדִּבּוּר.

---

35) Where in Egypt is Joseph buried?
36) Where is Moses buried?
37) Where in Goshen was Jacob buried?

FORCED HIM TO GO DOWN TO EGYPT

We all know, though we are often loathe to admit it, that greatness in life is forged in the face of adversity. Somehow it is those formative life experiences that come as the blow from a sculptor's hammer and chisel—and not the painter's soft strokes—upon which we reflect with the deepest sense of satisfaction. Great mothers are molded more by the difficulties they encounter raising their children, then by the times their little ones behave like "perfect angels." We comfort and empathize with those who have suffered, while we revere those who triumph in the face of disaster.

No, we never wish accidents, illness, or even flat tires, missed appointments or stained ties on anyone. Yet we know that the trials of life, both great and small, are where superior quality of character and living are ultimately fashioned.

"God created circumstances that forced him..." We often have little control over the circumstances of our lives and the situations with which we are confronted. There is divine orchestration in life. Our role—our shot at freedom—is to address the conditions of our lives and to respond to all that comes our way with the type of dignity, maturity, and courage that makes us better human beings for having passed that way.

Guess What?

Pretty soon we're going to be at the ten plagues part of the seder and some really neat stuff is going to happen. I sure hope that whoever is leading your seder read the part in the introduction about how to make the ten plagues totally fun. If he didn't, then tell him you're going to steal his afikomen forever if he doesn't read it and come up with some quick ideas.
On second thought, don't threaten the poor guy, it's tough enough leading a seder. Try asking nicely, it usually works better.

Sojourned there– this teaches us that our father Jacob did not intend to settle in Egypt, rather to reside there on a temporary basis. This becomes even clearer when we look at another verse in the Torah that says, "Jacob's sons said to Pharaoh: "We have come to stay in this land for a while because a famine has struck the land of Israel and there is no where left to pasture our sheep. So please, let us, your servants, stay in the Egyptian district of Goshen."

Jacob and his small family– The size of Jacob's family is indicated to us when the Torah says; "With seventy soul(s), your ancestors descended to Egypt, and now God, has made you as numerous as the stars of heaven.

וַיָּגָר שָׁם—מְלַמֵּד שֶׁלֹּא יָרַד יַעֲקֹב אָבִינוּ לְהִשְׁתַּקֵּעַ בְּמִצְרַיִם, אֶלָּא לָגוּר שָׁם. שֶׁנֶּאֱמַר, וַיֹּאמְרוּ אֶל פַּרְעֹה, לָגוּר בָּאָרֶץ בָּאנוּ כִּי אֵין מִרְעֶה לַצֹּאן אֲשֶׁר לַעֲבָדֶיךָ, כִּי כָבֵד הָרָעָב בְּאֶרֶץ כְּנָעַן, וְעַתָּה יֵשְׁבוּ נָא עֲבָדֶיךָ בְּאֶרֶץ גֹּשֶׁן:

בִּמְתֵי מְעָט—כְּמָה שֶׁנֶּאֱמַר, בְּשִׁבְעִים נֶפֶשׁ יָרְדוּ אֲבֹתֶיךָ מִצְרָיְמָה, וְעַתָּה שָׂמְךָ יְהוָה אֱלֹהֶיךָ כְּכוֹכְבֵי הַשָּׁמַיִם לָרֹב:

With seventy soul(s) your ancestors

Wise Child: It says here that the Jews went down to Egypt *"with seventy soul."* Shouldn't it say "seventy souls," in the plural form, instead of the singular?

Answer: The singular use of the word "soul," points us to an essential quality that enabled the Jewish people to flourish in the monstrous pit of Egypt. In so doing, it also sheds some light on the dynamics of spiritual attainment.

Imagine a community whose relationship revolves around a common vow to similar ideals, aspirations and goals. To the spiritual aim of transforming the mundane into the meaningful, and daily routines into tiny lights of inspiration.

This was the family of Jacob—the nascent Jewish nation—that *"descended"* into the abyss of Egypt. Each family member possessed his or her own personality and perspective; each had a distinctive nature and style. They were strikingly individual, yet possessed of a common "soul" that drew them together into a striving, caring, and non-judgmental community.

In describing the Egyptians, our sages tell us that their cruelty was only surpassed by an unfettered addiction to everything lewd and degrading. At the same time we are told that *chesed*, the trait of kindness, sharing and sensitivity, was an aspect of Jewish life that never weakened in Egypt. That our people were redeemed from bondage was one miracle, that any trace of humanity and spirituality remained was quite another.

Surely this was a portent of things to come. The Jewish people is a nation of families and a family that is a nation. We are a people that has been forced to endure not only the most heinous physical abuses, but the simultaneous crushing force of a world that seeks to rob us of character, dignity, and sanity itself. There is only one road to survival. As one soul: Insisting upon our mandated right to strive for everything that lifts our hearts and inspires our souls.

38) When Jacob settled in Egypt, how large was his family?
39) Why is there a roasted bone on the seder plate?
40) In what month were the Jewish people freed from Egypt?
41) Can you name all of the Jewish months?
42) How long were the Jews slaves in Egypt?

There he became a nation– this implies that the Jews in Egypt, even before they were enslaved, maintained a distinctive identity. The Jews lived and even dressed differently from their Egyptian neighbors.

Great, powerful– as it says elsewhere in the Torah; "And the Jewish people were fruitful. They had many children, increased greatly, multiplied, and became very, very powerful; and the land of Egypt was filled with them."

Numerous– The Torah uses the imagery of a young child who has now grown up to describe what happened to the Jews in Egypt. As it says; "I enabled you to grow as numerous as the plants of the field; and you grew tall and became very successful and prosperous. You became charming and beautiful and your hair was long; yet, at the same time it was as if you were naked and bare. Physically you were beautiful, but spiritually you were lacking something. It was as if your soul had no clothes and was bleeding. So I introduced you to two mitzvot (commandments), both of which were related to blood. The mitzvah of circumcision and the mitzvah of the Passover Offering. And then I said to you: *The mitzvot are a source of life: And these mitzvot involving blood will be a source of life.*"

וַיְהִי שָׁם לְגוֹי– מְלַמֵּד שֶׁהָיוּ יִשְׂרָאֵל מְצֻיָּנִים שָׁם:

גָּדוֹל עָצוּם– כְּמָה שֶׁנֶּאֱמַר, וּבְנֵי יִשְׂרָאֵל פָּרוּ וַיִּשְׁרְצוּ וַיִּרְבּוּ וַיַּעַצְמוּ בִּמְאֹד מְאֹד, וַתִּמָּלֵא הָאָרֶץ אֹתָם:

וָרָב– כְּמָה שֶׁנֶּאֱמַר, רְבָבָה כְּצֶמַח הַשָּׂדֶה נְתַתִּיךְ, וַתִּרְבִּי וַתִּגְדְּלִי וַתָּבֹאִי בַּעֲדִי עֲדָיִים שָׁדַיִם נָכֹנוּ וּשְׂעָרֵךְ צִמֵּחַ וְאַתְּ עֵרֹם וְעֶרְיָה. וָאֶעֱבֹר עָלַיִךְ וָאֶרְאֵךְ מִתְבּוֹסֶסֶת בְּדָמָיִךְ, וָאֹמַר לָךְ בְּדָמַיִךְ חֲיִי, וָאֹמַר לָךְ בְּדָמַיִךְ חֲיִי:

AND THEY BECAME VERY, VERY POWERFUL

My daughter likes to roll up her sleeve, snap her arm into position, and challenge anyone within earshot: "Feel my muscle."

But what about us? Those of us who grapple with an interminable expansion of waistline, and who have traded in our war-torn jogging shoes for a more sedate pair of Air Walkers—what evidence can we produce that we too are the proprietors of enviable strength?

Our tradition teaches that true strength, is inner strength. To admit that you've made a mistake—that takes strength. To stand with a friend while others stand by laughing—that takes strength. To deal honestly where deception would be more lucrative—now that takes strength. The "power" that was cultivated in Egypt was the power of inner convictions.

We are now going to examine three more verses in the Torah that reveal in great detail what happened during the time when our people were slaves in Egypt. First the Haggadah will quote each verse in it's entirety, and then it will break the verse into it's component parts to high-light various insights and details.

This type of study can be a little difficult at first if you are not used to it. But don't worry, Jews have been doing this for thousands of years, and with a bit of patience I'm sure you'll catch on.

(I) *The Egyptians did evil to us; they afflicted us, made us suffer and imposed back-breaking labor on us.* (Deuteronomy 26:6).

The Egyptians did evil to us– the Torah tells us that the Egyptians said; "We better be very careful with these Jews and make sure we outsmart them, because if we don't, there will end up being so many of them that they will become a threat. If there is a war they might side with our enemies, fight against us and then flee the country."

They afflicted us– as the Torah says; "The Egyptians placed taskmasters over the Jews in order to oppress them with harsh labor; and the Jewish slaves built the treasure cities of Pithom and Ramses for Pharaoh."

And imposed backbreaking labor on us– as it says in the Torah; "The Egyptians forced brutally difficult work on the Jewish slaves."

(II) *We cried out to the God of our ancestors; and God heard our voice and saw our affliction, our burden, and our oppression.* (Deuteronomy 26:7).

We cried out to the God of our ancestors– as the Torah says; "It happened after a long time that the king of Egypt died; and the Jewish people groaned because of the oppressive work and they cried out in distress; and the crying caused by the work went up to God."

God heard our voice– as it says; "God heard the bitter groaning of the Jewish slaves, and God reflected upon His covenant with Abraham, with Isaac and with Jacob."

וַיָּרֵעוּ אֹתָנוּ הַמִּצְרִים וַיְעַנּוּנוּ וַיִּתְּנוּ עָלֵינוּ עֲבֹדָה קָשָׁה:

וַיָּרֵעוּ אֹתָנוּ הַמִּצְרִים—כְּמָה שֶׁנֶּאֱמַר, הָבָה נִתְחַכְּמָה לוֹ פֶּן יִרְבֶּה וְהָיָה כִּי תִקְרֶאנָה מִלְחָמָה וְנוֹסַף גַּם הוּא עַל־שֹׂנְאֵינוּ וְנִלְחַם בָּנוּ, וְעָלָה מִן הָאָרֶץ:

וַיְעַנּוּנוּ—כְּמָה שֶׁנֶּאֱמַר, וַיָּשִׂימוּ עָלָיו שָׂרֵי מִסִּים לְמַעַן עַנֹּתוֹ בְּסִבְלֹתָם, וַיִּבֶן עָרֵי מִסְכְּנוֹת לְפַרְעֹה, אֶת־פִּתֹם וְאֶת־רַעַמְסֵס:

וַיִּתְּנוּ עָלֵינוּ עֲבֹדָה קָשָׁה— כְּמָה שֶׁנֶּאֱמַר, וַיַּעֲבִדוּ מִצְרַיִם אֶת־בְּנֵי יִשְׂרָאֵל בְּפָרֶךְ:

וַנִּצְעַק אֶל־יְהֹוָה אֱלֹהֵי אֲבוֹתֵינוּ, וַיִּשְׁמַע יְהֹוָה אֶת־קֹלֵנוּ, וַיַּרְא אֶת־עָנְיֵנוּ, וְאֶת־עֲמָלֵנוּ וְאֶת־לַחֲצֵנוּ:

וַנִּצְעַק אֶל־יְהֹוָה אֱלֹהֵי אֲבוֹתֵינוּ—כְּמָה שֶׁנֶּאֱמַר, וַיְהִי בַיָּמִים הָרַבִּים הָהֵם וַיָּמָת מֶלֶךְ מִצְרַיִם, וַיֵּאָנְחוּ בְנֵי יִשְׂרָאֵל מִן הָעֲבֹדָה וַיִּזְעָקוּ, וַתַּעַל שַׁוְעָתָם אֶל־הָאֱלֹהִים מִן הָעֲבֹדָה:

וַיִּשְׁמַע יְהֹוָה אֶת־קֹלֵנוּ—כְּמָה שֶׁנֶּאֱמַר, וַיִּשְׁמַע אֱלֹהִים אֶת־נַאֲקָתָם, וַיִּזְכֹּר אֱלֹהִים אֶת־בְּרִיתוֹ אֶת־אַבְרָהָם, אֶת־יִצְחָק, וְאֶת־יַעֲקֹב:

THE EGYPTIANS WERE VERY BAD TO US
AND THEY MADE US SUFFER

Fifty years ago there was a terrible war. This war was called World War Two. WWII was started by a country called Germany, that elected a very evil leader named Adolf Hitler. The Germans wanted to do two things. They wanted to conquer other countries in Europe, and they wanted to kill all the Jews who lived in Europe. Eventually Germany was defeated, but by the time the war was over they had succeeded in killing almost all the Jews of Europe, including more than one million Jewish children.

Sometimes it's hard to imagine how people can be so cruel to other people. How could the Egyptians have been so cruel three thousand years ago, and how could the German people have been so cruel just fifty years ago?

This is a true story told by an American soldier who fought against the Germans in WWII. His name is Sergeant Bill.

"After the war was over and Germany had been defeated, the Americans established temporary local military governments in many German cities. It was our job to try and get these cities functioning again. I had served in the 97th Infantry Division under General Patton and was assigned to work as a small town on the outskirts of Pilsen."

"One day I was walking near a stream and I saw two German teenage girls playing there." 'Where do you live?' I asked them. 'We used to live in Berlin, but now we live here.' 'And why did your family move here?' I asked. 'Because Hitler gave our father the shoe factory here,' they said. 'And where did Hitler get the factory from?' 'The Jews,' they answered. 'He took it from the Jews and he gave it to our father.' 'And where is your house?' I continued to ask. "That's our house over there,' they said, pointing to a beautiful home, 'Hitler gave us that too.'

'How do you feel about living in a house that was taken away from another family?' I asked. 'They were just Jews,' was their innocent reply. 'I know, but how would you feel if someone came and took your things and gave them away to someone else?' They looked at me with a funny sort of look and repeated their answer, 'They were just Jews.'

Most people would never want to cause other people to suffer. In Egypt and Germany, Jews stopped being looked at as people. Instead, they were "just Jews."

And saw our affliction– this refers to the disruption of normal family life, as it says; "God saw what was happening to the Jewish people. God was imminently aware of the pain in every home and He was poised to act."

Our burden– this refers to the children, as it says; "Pharaoh commanded that every newborn son be thrown into the river, but every daughter would be allowed to live."

Our oppression– this refers to the unrelenting pressure, as indicated by the words; "I have also seen how the Egyptians apply constant pressure and never give the Jews a moment to relax."

(III) *God brought us out of Egypt with a strong hand and with an outstretched arm, with great awe, with signs and with wonders.* (Deuteronomy 26:8).

God brought us out of Egypt– When it came time to rescue the Jews from Egypt, God did not work through any kind of intermediary, angel or representative. Rather, God Himself rescued us and that is exactly how if felt; as if God were personally clearing the way for us to leave. In this regard the Torah says; "I will pass through the land of Egypt on that night and I will slay every firstborn in Egypt, both people and animals; and I will demonstrate that all the idols and gods of the Egyptians are utterly powerless: It will be absolutely clear that there is only One God."

When God said, "I will pass through the land of Egypt on that night," He was saying that He would not use any intermediary and that His actual presence would be clearly manifest.

When God said, "I will slay every firstborn in Egypt," it was as if He said, "I will not send an angel, rather, I will do this Myself."

When God said, "I will demonstrate that all the idols and gods of the Egyptians are utterly powerless," it was as if He said, "I Myself will make this perfectly clear, and I will certainly not appoint a representative to demonstrate this critical lesson."

When God said, "it will be absolutely clear that there is only One God," it was as if He said, "I am the life source of all existence, only I can do all this, no one else."

וַיַּרְא אֶת־עָנְיֵנוּ — זוֹ פְּרִישׁוּת דֶּרֶךְ אֶרֶץ, כְּמָה שֶׁנֶּאֱמַר, וַיַּרְא אֱלֹהִים אֶת־בְּנֵי יִשְׂרָאֵל וַיֵּדַע אֱלֹהִים:

וְאֶת־עֲמָלֵנוּ — אֵלוּ הַבָּנִים, כְּמָה שֶׁנֶּאֱמַר, כָּל הַבֵּן הַיִּלּוֹד הַיְאֹרָה תַּשְׁלִיכֻהוּ וְכָל־הַבַּת תְּחַיּוּן:

וְאֶת־לַחֲצֵנוּ — זֶה הַדְּחַק, כְּמָה שֶׁנֶּאֱמַר, וְגַם רָאִיתִי אֶת־הַלַּחַץ אֲשֶׁר מִצְרַיִם לֹחֲצִים אֹתָם:

וַיּוֹצִאֵנוּ יְהוָֹה מִמִּצְרַיִם בְּיָד חֲזָקָה וּבִזְרֹעַ נְטוּיָה וּבְמֹרָא גָּדֹל וּבְאֹתֹת וּבְמֹפְתִים:

וַיּוֹצִאֵנוּ יְהוָֹה מִמִּצְרַיִם — לֹא עַל יְדֵי מַלְאָךְ, וְלֹא עַל יְדֵי שָׂרָף, וְלֹא עַל יְדֵי שָׁלִיחַ, אֶלָּא הַקָּדוֹשׁ בָּרוּךְ הוּא בִּכְבוֹדוֹ וּבְעַצְמוֹ. שֶׁנֶּאֱמַר, וְעָבַרְתִּי בְאֶרֶץ מִצְרַיִם בַּלַּיְלָה הַזֶּה וְהִכֵּיתִי כָל־בְּכוֹר בְּאֶרֶץ מִצְרַיִם מֵאָדָם וְעַד בְּהֵמָה, וּבְכָל־אֱלֹהֵי מִצְרַיִם אֶעֱשֶׂה שְׁפָטִים אֲנִי יְהוָֹה: וְעָבַרְתִּי בְאֶרֶץ מִצְרַיִם, אֲנִי וְלֹא מַלְאָךְ. וְהִכֵּיתִי כָל בְּכוֹר בְּאֶרֶץ מִצְרַיִם, אֲנִי וְלֹא שָׂרָף. וּבְכָל אֱלֹהֵי מִצְרַיִם אֶעֱשֶׂה שְׁפָטִים, אֲנִי וְלֹא הַשָּׁלִיחַ. אֲנִי יְהוָֹה. אֲנִי הוּא, וְלֹא אַחֵר:

THIS REFERS TO THE UNRELENTING PRESSURE

We're under a lot of pressure. Just look at people, or yourself, and see if it doesn't seem as if some indomitable boss is standing over us all, making sure that every minute is a busy minute.

According to the eighteenth-century philosopher and mystic, Rabbi Moshe Chaim Luzzatto, there actually is such a boss. And this boss, this hovering prince of pressure, is symbolized by none other than Pharaoh himself. Conceptually, Pharaoh is the embodiment of everything oppressive.

Rabbi Luzzatto speaks of a force that seeks to wreak havoc in our lives simply by never giving us a moment's rest. For if given time to rest and reflect, Pharaoh knows that his days as a slave driver would soon be over. Pharaoh's arch-enemy, the champion of freedom and spirituality; is quiet contemplation.

With a strong hand– this is referring to the plague of pestilence that killed the Egyptians animals, as the Torah says; "The hand of God will strike your cattle that are in the field; the horses, the donkeys, the camels, the herds, and the flocks–the plague of pestilence will be very severe."

With an outstretched arm– the word "outstretched" is an allusion to the death of many Egyptians. We know that the term outstretched has this connotation because once there was a plague that killed thousands of people in Jerusalem and there the Torah says, "And His sword is drawn in his hand, it is outstretched over Jerusalem."

With great awe– this alludes to the obvious fact of God's direct involvement in rescuing the Jews, and the overwhelming sense of awe one feels when they realize they are in the presence of God, as the Torah says; "Did God ever intervene in history and take one nation from the midst of another nation; by signs, wonders, miracles and by war, with a strong hand, an outstretched arm and with an awesome display of force? This has happened to no other people in history, but it did happen to your people in Egypt, before your very own eyes."

With signs– this refers to the staff that Moses used when he was sent by God to perform the miracles, as it says; "Take this staff in your hand, so that you may perform the signs with it."

With wonders– this is a reference to the plague of blood, as it says; "I will display wonders in the sky and on the ground." (i.e. a river will turn to blood).

בְּיָד חֲזָקָה—זֶה הַדֶּבֶר כְּמָה שֶׁנֶּאֱמַר, הִנֵּה יַד יְהוָה הוֹיָה בְּמִקְנְךָ אֲשֶׁר בַּשָּׂדֶה, בַּסּוּסִים בַּחֲמֹרִים בַּגְּמַלִּים בַּבָּקָר וּבַצֹּאן, דֶּבֶר כָּבֵד מְאֹד:

וּבִזְרֹעַ נְטוּיָה—זוֹ הַחֶרֶב, כְּמָה שֶׁנֶּאֱמַר, וְחַרְבּוֹ שְׁלוּפָה בְּיָדוֹ, נְטוּיָה עַל יְרוּשָׁלָיִם.

וּבְמֹרָא גָּדֹל—זֶה גִּלּוּי שְׁכִינָה, כְּמָה שֶׁנֶּאֱמַר, אוֹ הֲנִסָּה אֱלֹהִים לָבֹא לָקַחַת לוֹ גוֹי מִקֶּרֶב גּוֹי בְּמַסֹּת, בְּאֹתֹת, וּבְמוֹפְתִים, וּבְמִלְחָמָה, וּבְיָד חֲזָקָה, וּבִזְרֹעַ נְטוּיָה , וּבְמוֹרָאִים גְּדוֹלִים, כְּכֹל אֲשֶׁר עָשָׂה לָכֶם יְהוָה אֱלֹהֵיכֶם בְּמִצְרַיִם לְעֵינֶיךָ:

וּבְאֹתוֹת— זֶה הַמַּטֶה, כְּמָה שֶׁנֶּאֱמַר, וְאֶת־הַמַּטֶה הַזֶּה תִּקַּח בְּיָדֶךָ, אֲשֶׁר
תַּעֲשֶׂה־בּוֹ אֶת־הָאֹתוֹת: וּבְמוֹפְתִים—זֶה הַדָּם, כְּמָה שֶׁנֶּאֱמַר, וְנָתַתִּי מוֹפְתִים
בַּשָּׁמַיִם וּבָאָרֶץ:

Take this staff in your hand...

Wise Child: Why did God tell Moses to hold a staff in his hand before initiating the plagues?

Answer: One of the most serious obstacles to bringing one's potential to fruition is what Judaism calls *ya'ush*—utter despair. *Ya'ush* sounds the doleful lament of one who sees inescapable limitations and recurrent failings as proof that all the future holds is the drudgery of survival at best, or bitter failure at worst. *Ya'ush* sets in when one finally accepts that he or she will never achieve anything of significance and will never "amount to anything."

The message of the staff is one that calls on us to bravely stand-up to *ya'ush*—to despairing of one's abilities and potential—and to boldly insist that our lives are still ours to live.

On the surface, the staff of Moses was nothing more than a piece of dead wood. We can almost hear ourselves saying, "there is about as much chance of me changing myself, let alone the world, as there is of a stick being able to turn a river into blood." But that is exactly what happened.

The staff urges us to look beneath the surface and to connect with the deepest part of ourselves; our souls. To detect the hidden rumblings of potential where there seems to be none. In ourselves, as well as in others. In children, students, friends, spouses, and even in the Jewish people. Leave no stone unturned in this search for reservoirs of strength and capability. Discover them, value them, and carefully nurture them. And know—each in our own way— we can make a difference. We can accomplish and contribute, and above all, we can override the clutches of despair and once again begin to grow.

We now do something to highlight the fact that in rescuing the Jewish people from Egypt, God performed "wonders" both in the sky and on the ground. The upcoming declaration of the word *blood*, relates to the wonder that affected the ground (the river turning to blood), while the declaration of the words *fire* and *pillars of smoke*, relate to those things that affected the sky and the air.

As each of the following words; blood, fire, and pillars of smoke, is said, a bit of wine is removed from the cup, either with a finger or by pouring.

Blood — Fire — And Pillars of Smoke

We have now completed our examination of the three verses from the Torah. However, before we go further, we are going to look at a brief alternative explanation of the third verse. According to this alternative explanation, each of the highlighted words or phrases in the verse represents two of the ten plagues. Let's take a look:

Mighty hand– these two words represent two plagues. **Outstretched arm**– again; two words, two plagues. **Great awe**– two words, two plagues. **Signs**– One word, however in the plural form, this also represents two plagues. **Wonders**– again, the plural form represents two plagues.

When taken together these five phrases correspond to the ten plagues that God used to force the Egyptians to finally let the Jewish people go.

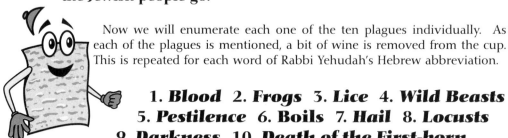

Now we will enumerate each one of the ten plagues individually. As each of the plagues is mentioned, a bit of wine is removed from the cup. This is repeated for each word of Rabbi Yehudah's Hebrew abbreviation.

1. *Blood* 2. *Frogs* 3. *Lice* 4. *Wild Beasts* 5. *Pestilence* 6. *Boils* 7. *Hail* 8. *Locusts* 9. *Darkness* 10. *Death of the First-born*

131
PSK

Hooray!!

Rabbi Judah abbreviated the plagues by using a mnemonic comprised of the first Hebrew letter of each plague. In this way he divided the plagues into three groups.

(I) D'TZACH,	**(II) ADASH,**	**(III) B'ACHAB**
(1,2,3)	(4,5,6)	(7,8,9,10)

The cups are refilled with fresh wine to replace what was removed.

דָּם, וָאֵשׁ, וְתִמְרוֹת עָשָׁן:

דָּבָר אַחֵר: בְּיָד חֲזָקָה, שְׁתַּיִם. וּבִזְרוֹעַ נְטוּיָה, שְׁתַּיִם. וּבְמוֹרָא גָדוֹל, שְׁתַּיִם. וּבְאֹתוֹת, שְׁתַּיִם. וּבְמֹפְתִים, שְׁתַּיִם: אֵלּוּ עֶשֶׂר מַכּוֹת שֶׁהֵבִיא הַקָּדוֹשׁ בָּרוּךְ הוּא עַל הַמִּצְרִים בְּמִצְרָיִם. וְאֵלּוּ הֵן:

דָּם.
צְפַרְדֵּעַ. כִּנִּים. עָרוֹב. דֶּבֶר. שְׁחִין. בָּרָד. אַרְבֶּה.
חֹשֶׁךְ. מַכַּת בְּכוֹרוֹת:

רַבִּי יְהוּדָה הָיָה נוֹתֵן בָּהֶם סִמָּנִים:

דְּצַ"ךְ. עֲדַ"שׁ. בְּאַחַ"ב:

---

43) What was unusual about the plague of blood?
44) What was unusual about the plague of hail?
45) Why did Aaron and not Moses perform the plague of blood?
46) Why do we spill out some wine when we recite the ten plagues?
47) What happened seven weeks after the Jews left Egypt?

Now that we have been introduced to the ten plagues, we are going to take a second look at them. The following discussion contains the opinion of three great Talmudic sages. As we will see, all three sages were of the opinion that the Egyptians were the victims of many more than just ten plagues. However, they differed when it came to the exact number of plagues that took place. First we will get an overview of the three opinions and then we will examine each one in detail.

OVERVIEW

1) Rabbi Yossi of Galilee. His opinion is that all together there were sixty plagues. Ten in Egypt and then another fifty which struck the Egyptians when they chased the Jews into the Red Sea. (60).

2) Rabbi Eliezer. He says that each plague actually contained four different plagues within it. Therefore, instead of ten plagues in Egypt there were actually forty plagues. And, instead of fifty plagues at the sea, there were really two hundred. All together there were two hundred and forty plagues. (240).

3) Rabbi Akiva. He says that each plague actually contained five plagues. Thus, there were fifty plagues in Egypt and two hundred and fifty at the sea, for a total of three hundred plagues. (300).

DETAILED ANALYSIS

1) Rabbi Yossi of Galilee said: If we examine the words of the Torah carefully, we will see that God inflicted five times as many plagues on the Egyptians at the Red Sea as He did in Egypt. Regarding the plagues in Egypt the Torah says; The magicians said to Pharaoh, 'It is the finger of God.' However when it comes to the sea, the Torah says; "Israel saw the great hand which God brought against the Egyptians, and the people were in awe of God; and they trusted both God and in His servant Moses." We know that in Egypt there were ten plagues and we see that the Torah refers to them as the finger of God? In that case when the Torah refers to the hand of God, at the sea, it must mean that there were five times as many plagues at the sea. So we can calculate that if they were struck by ten plagues in Egypt (where the instrument was a finger), they must have been struck by fifty plagues at the sea (where the instrument was a whole hand).

2) Rabbi Eliezer said: Rabbi Yossi is correct about there being more plagues at the sea than in Egypt, however the total

number of plagues was even greater than he thinks. If we examine the words of the Torah we will see that each plague had four different parts to it. The Torah says, "He sent upon them His fierce anger [in the form of] **wrath, fury, trouble** and **emissaries of evil**" The implication of this verse is that each plague contained four elements: 1) **wrath**, 2) **fury**, 3) **trouble** and, 4) **emissaries of evil**; therefore we can calculate that in Egypt they were struck by forty plagues (10x4), and at the sea by two hundred plagues (50x4). Together this means that there were two hundred and forty plagues.

3) **Rabbi Akiva said:** The verse in the Torah that Rabbi Eliezer quoted should be read a little differently. According to Rabbi Eliezer each of the plagues is termed "fierce anger," and then he divides each fierce anger/plague into four parts. In fact, fierce anger is more than just a synonym for plague, rather it is a fifth element contained within each of the plagues. The verse should be read as follows; "He sent upon them His **fierce anger, wrath, fury, trouble,** and **emissaries of evil**." Each plague in Egypt thus contained five elements; 1) **fierce anger**, 2) **wrath**, 3) **fury**, 4) **trouble** and, 5) **emissaries of evil**, therefore we can calculate that in Egypt they were struck by fifty plagues (10x5), and at the sea by two hundred and fifty plagues (50x5). Together this means that there were a total of three hundred plagues.

Ten plagues... forty plagues... two hundred and fifty plagues...

Rebellious Child: Who cares how many plagues there were? God did a bunch of miracles to free the Jews and that's all we need to know.

Answer: At the conclusion of a delicious dinner when a child says, "thanks mom," before running outside, or when his father says, "thank you dear," before grabbing the paper, the question is this: How thankful are those guys anyway?

A sincere expression of gratitude draws both benefactor and provider closer together. Every married couple needs to know that a vivid recollection of kindness bestowed is a powerful way to draw two hearts together.

Think about all the effort that goes into the average dinner. It begins with someone thinking about which foods will be both nutritious and tasty. This is followed by a look in the fridge to check what ingredients are not on hand, the composition of a shopping list, and the drive (at times in the nastiest of weather) to the grocery store. After numerous trips up and down the aisles—searching for just the right ingredients at just the right price—there comes the trip home. A trip that ends with shlepping in the heavy bags and putting everything away. All this precedes various types of preparation—from boiling water to dicing vegetables; the cooking, and then the clean-up.

From this bird's-eye view we can begin to see that the list of kindnesses and efforts involved in many of the daily deeds from which we benefit—and tend to take for granted—is remarkably long.

The more carefully we consider each aspect of what someone has done for us, the closer and more connected we will feel. Earnest gratitude will draw our hearts close: to our parents, our spouses, and to the Almighty as well.

רַבִּי יוֹסֵי הַגְּלִילִי אוֹמֵר: מִנַּיִן אַתָּה אוֹמֵר שֶׁלָּקוּ הַמִּצְרִים בְּמִצְרַיִם עֶשֶׂר מַכּוֹת וְעַל הַיָּם לָקוּ חֲמִשִּׁים מַכּוֹת? בְּמִצְרַיִם מַה הוּא אוֹמֵר, וַיֹּאמְרוּ הַחַרְטֻמִּים אֶל־פַּרְעֹה, אֶצְבַּע אֱלֹהִים הִיא. וְעַל הַיָּם מַה הוּא אוֹמֵר, וַיַּרְא יִשְׂרָאֵל אֶת־הַיָּד הַגְּדֹלָה אֲשֶׁר עָשָׂה יְהֹוָה בְּמִצְרַיִם וַיִּירְאוּ הָעָם אֶת־יְהֹוָה וַיַּאֲמִינוּ בַּיהֹוָה וּבְמֹשֶׁה עַבְדּוֹ: כַּמָּה לָקוּ בְאֶצְבַּע? עֶשֶׂר מַכּוֹת. אֱמֹר מֵעַתָּה, בְּמִצְרַיִם לָקוּ עֶשֶׂר מַכּוֹת, וְעַל הַיָּם לָקוּ חֲמִשִּׁים מַכּוֹת:

רַבִּי אֱלִיעֶזֶר אוֹמֵר: מִנַּיִן שֶׁכָּל־מַכָּה וּמַכָּה שֶׁהֵבִיא הַקָּדוֹשׁ בָּרוּךְ הוּא עַל הַמִּצְרִים בְּמִצְרַיִם הָיְתָה שֶׁל אַרְבַּע מַכּוֹת? שֶׁנֶּאֱמַר, יְשַׁלַּח בָּם חֲרוֹן אַפּוֹ— עֶבְרָה, וָזַעַם, וְצָרָה, מִשְׁלַחַת מַלְאֲכֵי רָעִים: עֶבְרָה, אַחַת. וָזַעַם, שְׁתַּיִם. וְצָרָה, שָׁלֹשׁ. מִשְׁלַחַת מַלְאֲכֵי רָעִים, אַרְבַּע. אֱמֹר מֵעַתָּה, בְּמִצְרַיִם לָקוּ אַרְבָּעִים מַכּוֹת, וְעַל הַיָּם לָקוּ מָאתַיִם מַכּוֹת:

רַבִּי עֲקִיבָא אוֹמֵר: מִנַּיִן שֶׁכָּל־מַכָּה וּמַכָּה שֶׁהֵבִיא הַקָּדוֹשׁ בָּרוּךְ הוּא עַל הַמִּצְרִים בְּמִצְרַיִם הָיְתָה שֶׁל חָמֵשׁ מַכּוֹת? שֶׁנֶּאֱמַר, יְשַׁלַּח בָּם חֲרוֹן אַפּוֹ, עֶבְרָה, וָזַעַם, וְצָרָה, מִשְׁלַחַת מַלְאֲכֵי רָעִים: חֲרוֹן אַפּוֹ, אַחַת. עֶבְרָה, שְׁתַּיִם. וָזַעַם, שָׁלֹשׁ. וְצָרָה, אַרְבַּע. מִשְׁלַחַת מַלְאֲכֵי רָעִים, חָמֵשׁ. אֱמֹר מֵעַתָּה, בְּמִצְרַיִם לָקוּ חֲמִשִּׁים מַכּוֹת, וְעַל הַיָּם לָקוּ חֲמִשִּׁים וּמָאתַיִם מַכּוֹת:

Mazel Tov! We have just completed the main portion of the Haggadah text. For most of the rest of the seder we will be involved in some very special, and tasty mitzvot. Soon we will be eating matzah and maror as well as the Hillel matzah sandwich. And then; we're on to the main meal–and that's a mitzvah too! So get ready, because there is some great stuff waiting for us just around the corner.

The last part of the Haggadah that we read contained a brief summary of what took place in Egypt. We saw how the Jews were enslaved and brutally oppressed. We saw how in their time of anguish and despair the Jews cried out to God. And we saw how God brought numerous plagues upon the Egyptians and finally rescued the Jewish people from their Egyptian oppressors.

It is now time for us to stop and reflect upon all that God did for our ancestors. The song Dayenu is meant to focus our attention not only on the big picture of being rescued, but on each and every aspect of what happened and each and every blessing that God gave to us as the Jewish people.

DAYENU

God has done an overwhelming number of favors for us! And we want to express our gratitude for each and every one.

**Had He just saved us from slavery in Egypt,
but not executed judgments against the Egyptians,
Dayenu –this would have been enough.
Had He just executed judgments against them,
but not showed their gods to be powerless,
Dayenu –this would have been enough.
Had He just shown their gods to be powerless,
but not killed their firstborn,
Dayenu –this would have been enough.
Had He just killed their firstborn,
but not given us their wealth,
Dayenu –this would have been enough.
Had He just given us their wealth,
but not split the sea for us,
Dayenu –this would have been enough.
Had He just split the sea for us,
but not led us across on dry land,
Dayenu –this would have been enough.
Had He just led us across on dry land,**

but not drowned the Egyptian army in the sea,
>   **Dayenu** –this would have been enough.

Had He just drowned the Egyptian army in the sea,
but not taken care of us in the desert for forty years,
>   **Dayenu** –this would have been enough.

Had He just taken care of us in the desert for forty years,
but not fed us the daily food called Manna,
>   **Dayenu** –this would have been enough.

Had He just fed us the daily food called Manna,
but not given us the Sabbath as a time for spirituality,
>   **Dayenu** –this would have been enough.

Had He just given us the Sabbath as a time for spirituality,
but not brought us to Mount Sinai,
>   **Dayenu** –this would have been enough.

Had He just brought us to Mount Sinai,
but not given us the Torah,
>   **Dayenu** –this would have been enough.

Had He just given us the Torah,
but not brought us into the Land of Israel,
>   **Dayenu** –this would have been enough.

Had he just brought us into the Land of Israel,
but not built the Temple in Jerusalem for us,
>   **Dayenu** –this would have been enough.

Since God actually did do all these wonderful favors for us, we should certainly be very grateful. Just look at the list of what was done for our people by God.

1) He saved us from a bitter slavery in Egypt.
2) He executed judgement on the Egyptians by afflicting them with terrible plagues.
3) He made it clear that the Egyptian gods were absolutely powerless.
4) He killed the firstborn of every Egyptian family.
5) He gave us the Egyptians wealth to take with us when we were saved.
6) He split the sea for us when we were cornered by the Egyptian army.
7) He led us across the sea on dry ground.
8) He drowned the stubborn Egyptian army that chased us into the sea.
9) He took care of us for forty years in the desert between

the time we left Egypt and when we eventually arrived in the Land of Israel.

10) He fed us a special food called Manna for the forty years that we were in the desert.

11) He gave us the Sabbath as a day of rest and spirituality.

12) He brought us to the foot of Mount Sinai.

13) He gave us the Torah; His instructions for living.

14) He brought us to our homeland; the Land of Israel.

15) He built the Temple in Jerusalem as a place where we could feel especially close to Him.

כַּמָּה מַעֲלוֹת טוֹבוֹת לַמָּקוֹם עָלֵינוּ:

אִלּוּ הוֹצִיאָנוּ מִמִּצְרַיִם, וְלֹא עָשָׂה בָהֶם שְׁפָטִים, דַּיֵּנוּ:

אִלּוּ עָשָׂה בָהֶם שְׁפָטִים, וְלֹא עָשָׂה בֵאלֹהֵיהֶם, דַּיֵּנוּ:

אִלּוּ עָשָׂה בֵאלֹהֵיהֶם, וְלֹא הָרַג אֶת-בְּכוֹרֵיהֶם, דַּיֵּנוּ:

אִלּוּ הָרַג אֶת-בְּכוֹרֵיהֶם, וְלֹא נָתַן לָנוּ אֶת-מָמוֹנָם, דַּיֵּנוּ:

אִלּוּ נָתַן לָנוּ אֶת-מָמוֹנָם, וְלֹא קָרַע לָנוּ אֶת-הַיָּם, דַּיֵּנוּ:

אִלּוּ קָרַע לָנוּ אֶת-הַיָּם, וְלֹא הֶעֱבִירָנוּ בְתוֹכוֹ בֶּחָרָבָה, דַּיֵּנוּ:

אִלּוּ הֶעֱבִירָנוּ בְתוֹכוֹ, בֶּחָרָבָה, וְלֹא שִׁקַּע צָרֵינוּ בְּתוֹכוֹ, דַּיֵּנוּ:

אִלּוּ שִׁקַּע צָרֵינוּ בְּתוֹכוֹ, וְלֹא סִפֵּק צָרְכֵּנוּ בַּמִּדְבָּר אַרְבָּעִים שָׁנָה, דַּיֵּנוּ:

אִלּוּ סִפֵּק צָרְכֵּנוּ בַּמִּדְבָּר אַרְבָּעִים שָׁנָה, וְלֹא הֶאֱכִילָנוּ אֶת-הַמָּן, דַּיֵּנוּ:

אִלּוּ הֶאֱכִילָנוּ אֶת-הַמָּן, וְלֹא נָתַן לָנוּ אֶת-הַשַּׁבָּת, דַּיֵּנוּ:

אִלּוּ נָתַן לָנוּ אֶת-הַשַּׁבָּת, וְלֹא קֵרְבָנוּ לִפְנֵי הַר-סִינַי, דַּיֵּנוּ:

אִלּוּ קֵרְבָנוּ לִפְנֵי הַר-סִינַי, וְלֹא נָתַן לָנוּ אֶת-הַתּוֹרָה, דַּיֵּנוּ:

אִלּוּ נָתַן לָנוּ אֶת-הַתּוֹרָה, וְלֹא הִכְנִיסָנוּ לְאֶרֶץ יִשְׂרָאֵל, דַּיֵּנוּ:

אִלּוּ הִכְנִיסָנוּ לְאֶרֶץ יִשְׂרָאֵל, וְלֹא בָנָה לָנוּ אֶת-בֵּית-הַבְּחִירָה, דַּיֵּנוּ:

עַל-אַחַת כַּמָּה וְכַמָּה טוֹבָה כְפוּלָה וּמְכֻפֶּלֶת לַמָּקוֹם עָלֵינוּ. שֶׁהוֹצִיאָנוּ מִמִּצְרַיִם. וְעָשָׂה בָהֶם שְׁפָטִים. וְעָשָׂה בֵאלֹהֵיהֶם. וְהָרַג אֶת-בְּכוֹרֵיהֶם. וְנָתַן לָנוּ אֶת-מָמוֹנָם. וְקָרַע לָנוּ אֶת-הַיָּם. וְהֶעֱבִירָנוּ בְתוֹכוֹ בֶּחָרָבָה. וְשִׁקַּע צָרֵינוּ בְּתוֹכוֹ. וְסִפֵּק צָרְכֵּנוּ בַּמִּדְבָּר אַרְבָּעִים שָׁנָה. וְהֶאֱכִילָנוּ אֶת-הַמָּן. וְנָתַן לָנוּ אֶת-הַשַּׁבָּת. וְקֵרְבָנוּ לִפְנֵי הַר-סִינַי. וְנָתַן לָנוּ אֶת-הַתּוֹרָה. וְהִכְנִיסָנוּ לְאֶרֶץ יִשְׂרָאֵל. וּבָנָה לָנוּ אֶת בֵּית-הַבְּחִירָה לְכַפֵּר עַל כָּל-עֲוֹנוֹתֵינוּ:

When the Temple stood in Jerusalem, it played a central role in the spiritual life of the Jewish nation. Whenever a Jew wanted to express special feelings of closeness to God, he or she could present an "offering" in the Temple. The Hebrew word for offering is *korban*. The word korban literally means, "to draw close." Three times a year; on Passover, Shavuot and Sukkot, Jews from all over Israel would gather at the Temple in Jerusalem to experience the inspiration of being a part of the Jewish people.

On Passover every Jewish family would bring a special offering to the Temple. This offering consisted of a lamb, and is known as the Korban Pesach, the Passover Offering. This special Passover lamb was eaten at the seder together with matzah and maror (bitter herbs).

The Haggadah will now begin a brief discussion about the Passover offering, the matzah and the maror.

Rabbi Gamliel used to say; Anyone who has not discussed the following three things on Passover has not fulfilled the basic obligation of the seder. The three things are: **Pesach (the Passover Offering)**; **Matzah**; and **Maror (the Bitter Herbs).**

25/69
ᴾ

Pesach—Why did our ancestors eat the Passover Offering in the days when we still had the Temple in Jerusalem?

Because the Hebrew word Pesach, means "to pass over," and the Passover Offering reminds us that when God killed the first-born of every Egyptian family, He passed over all the Jewish homes. This is what the Torah is referring to when it says; "You shall say: 'It is a Passover Offering for God, Who passed over the houses of the children of Israel in Egypt when He struck the Egyptians; as for our houses—they were spared: And the Jewish people bowed down as a sign of gratitude'.

The leader of the seder now lifts the middle matzah for all to see while the following paragraph is recited.

Matzah—Why do we eat the matzah?

Because when God took us out of Egypt, the end to our slavery came so quickly that there wasn't even time for our dough to rise. We just had to gather everything up and leave. This sudden departure is what the Torah is referring to when it says; "They baked the dough that they had brought out of Egypt into matzah because it had not risen; this was because they were driven out of Egypt. Not only did their dough not rise, but they didn't have a chance to prepare any other food."

The maror is lifted for everyone to see while the following paragraph is recited.

Maror—Why do we eat bitter herbs?

Because the Egyptian people made the lives of our ancestors very bitter, as it says in the Torah; "They embittered their lives with backbreaking labor, with mortar and bricks, with all sorts of jobs in the field; whatever labor they made them perform was excruciating."

רַבָּן גַּמְלִיאֵל הָיָה אוֹמֵר: כָּל־שֶׁלֹּא אָמַר שְׁלֹשָׁה דְבָרִים אֵלּוּ בַּפֶּסַח, לֹא יָצָא יְדֵי חוֹבָתוֹ. וְאֵלּוּ הֵן: פֶּסַח. מַצָּה. וּמָרוֹר:

פֶּסַח: שֶׁהָיוּ אֲבוֹתֵינוּ אוֹכְלִים בִּזְמַן שֶׁבֵּית־הַמִּקְדָּשׁ קַיָּם, עַל־שׁוּם מָה? עַל־שׁוּם שֶׁפָּסַח הַמָּקוֹם עַל־בָּתֵּי אֲבוֹתֵינוּ בְּמִצְרַיִם. שֶׁנֶּאֱמַר, וַאֲמַרְתֶּם זֶבַח פֶּסַח הוּא לַיהֹוָה אֲשֶׁר פָּסַח עַל־בָּתֵּי בְנֵי יִשְׂרָאֵל בְּמִצְרַיִם בְּנָגְפּוֹ אֶת־מִצְרַיִם, וְאֶת־בָּתֵּינוּ הִצִּיל וַיִּקֹּד הָעָם וַיִּשְׁתַּחֲווּ:

מַצָּה זוֹ: שֶׁאָנוּ אוֹכְלִים עַל־שׁוּם מָה? עַל־שׁוּם שֶׁלֹּא הִסְפִּיק בְּצֵקֶת שֶׁל אֲבוֹתֵינוּ לְהַחֲמִיץ עַד שֶׁנִּגְלָה עֲלֵיהֶם מֶלֶךְ מַלְכֵי הַמְּלָכִים הַקָּדוֹשׁ בָּרוּךְ הוּא וּגְאָלָם. שֶׁנֶּאֱמַר וַיֹּאפוּ אֶת־הַבָּצֵק אֲשֶׁר הוֹצִיאוּ מִמִּצְרַיִם עֻגֹת מַצּוֹת כִּי לֹא חָמֵץ כִּי גֹרְשׁוּ מִמִּצְרַיִם וְלֹא יָכְלוּ לְהִתְמַהְמֵהַּ וְגַם צֵדָה לֹא עָשׂוּ לָהֶם:

מָרוֹר זֶה: שֶׁאָנוּ אוֹכְלִים עַל־שׁוּם מָה? עַל־שׁוּם שֶׁמֵּרְרוּ הַמִּצְרִים אֶת־חַיֵּי אֲבוֹתֵינוּ בְּמִצְרַיִם. שֶׁנֶּאֱמַר, וַיְמָרְרוּ אֶת־חַיֵּיהֶם בַּעֲבֹדָה קָשָׁה, בְּחֹמֶר וּבִלְבֵנִים, וּבְכָל־עֲבֹדָה בַּשָּׂדֶה, אֵת כָּל־עֲבֹדָתָם אֲשֶׁר עָבְדוּ בָהֶם בְּפָרֶךְ:

48) Why don't we recline when we eat the maror?
49) How many times do you have to eat matzah during the seder?
50) Why don't we recline when we eat the matzah?

In every generation, each individual must see himself as though he personally had gone out of Egypt, as the Torah says; "You should tell your child on that day: 'It was because of these mitzvot (commandments), and because of our Jewish way of life, that God rescued *me* from Egypt.' It was not only our ancestors who were saved by God: We too were saved along with them. This is what the Torah means when it says; "He took *us* out of there so that He could take *us* to the land that He had promised to our ancestors; Abraham, Isaac and Jacob."

בְּכָל־דּוֹר וָדוֹר חַיָּב אָדָם לִרְאוֹת אֶת־עַצְמוֹ כְּאִלּוּ הוּא יָצָא מִמִּצְרָיִם. שֶׁנֶּאֱמַר, וְהִגַּדְתָּ לְבִנְךָ בַּיּוֹם הַהוּא לֵאמֹר, בַּעֲבוּר זֶה עָשָׂה יְהֹוָה לִי בְּצֵאתִי מִמִּצְרָיִם: לֹא אֶת־אֲבוֹתֵינוּ בִּלְבָד גָּאַל הַקָּדוֹשׁ בָּרוּךְ הוּא מִמִּצְרָיִם, אֶלָּא אַף אוֹתָנוּ גָּאַל עִמָּהֶם. שֶׁנֶּאֱמַר, וְאוֹתָנוּ הוֹצִיא מִשָּׁם, לְמַעַן הָבִיא אוֹתָנוּ לָתֶת לָנוּ אֶת־הָאָרֶץ אֲשֶׁר נִשְׁבַּע לַאֲבוֹתֵינוּ:

EACH INDIVIDUAL MUST SEE HIMSELF...

This statement identifies a central, though elusive goal of the entire seder experience. Namely, that on Passover, every Jew is to tingle with emotion as he or she rejoins the Jewish people at the original moment of redemption.

And just how is it that we—traveling through life with computers on our laps and phones in our cars—can hope to realistically achieve this experiential sensation of leaving ancient Egypt?

The key to this dilemma is two-fold. It is a mix of the painstaking, down-to-earth personal growth to which Passover calls us, with an almost mystical encounter with the ever-present soul of the Jewish people. In fact, this very paragraph hints to this convergence of past and present.

The first half of this paragraph speaks to us in the singular. "*A person... you should tell your son... G-d did for me,*" while the second half is in the plural. "*Not only our forefathers... we too were redeemed... in order to bring us.*"

This subtlety of language points to the two planes upon which we are to experience the freedom of Passover. As our hearts and minds engage the entirety of the seder, we are both dynamically autonomous individuals as well as molecular bits of the aggregate soul of the Jewish people.

As individuals, we wrestle with Egypt for our personal freedom. We initiate the type of introspection necessary to identify our essential goals, our arch impediments, and strategies for actualization. Without goals, freedom is an elusive tease. Without an awareness of entrenched deterrents, it's a fantasy. And without thoughtful generalship, it just won't happen.

Superimposed onto our personal strivings for freedom is our soul's linking up with an eternal spiritual dimension of existence known as *Klal Yisroel*, the Jewish people. It is to this dimension that our consciousness is drawn when the Haggadah speaks to us in the plural. *"Not only our forefathers did God redeem, but **we too** were redeemed with them."*

Our bodies die a million deaths as our cells silently decay and become mingled with the dust of history. Though most of the original me is long gone, *I* remain. The essence of self is a constant.

A '67 Chevy, though rebuilt from fender to fender, is still a '67 Chevy. And the same Klal Yisroel, the same Jewish nation that experienced the exodus from Egypt, is still alive today.

Tonight our personal quest for freedom, and the part of us that was present at the exodus, are fused together as one. And it is just this fusion that creates the potential to see ourselves as if we personally left Egypt.

37-43
פסח

51) What happened forty years after the Jews left Egypt?
52) What was the very first mitzvah that God told Moses to teach the Jewish people before they left Egypt?
53) Why do some families eat matzah ball soup at the seder?

The matzahs are covered, and the cup is lifted and held while the next three paragraphs are read.

Because of everything we have been speaking about tonight; the miracles and the incredible way that God saved us from Egypt and brought us to freedom, it is fitting that we express our abundant gratitude to the One who did all these things for our ancestors and for us.

He brought us from slavery to freedom, from sorrow to joy, from mourning to celebration, from darkness to radiant light, and from oppressive slavery to expansive freedom. When we reflect and take all of this to heart, we can't help but feel stirred to sing out a song of gratitude and praise!

Halleluyah! As Jews we are privileged to have a special relationship with God, and for this, we sing! We sing out our hope that the world always be aware of God; from the moment His fiery sun rises until it sets over the horizon. That all mankind will acknowledge God as the ultimate source of meaning, honor and spirituality. God is uniquely transcendent, yet he lowers Himself to look at the heaven and the earth. He gives the poor a sense of dignity, and He raises them from the dust; and the poverty stricken, He raises up from the trash heaps. He lifts the needy—to seat them with nobility, with the most respected of His nation. He transforms the barren wife into a joyous mother of children. Closeness to God is euphoric; and anything is possible. Halleluyah!

When our people, the nation of Israel—the house of Jacob— was saved from an alien people; a transformation took place. Now we would be a people whose identity is rooted in our relationship with God. The redemption of our people was an unprecedented event; it shook the world. The sea saw how we were freed, and split in front of us: As we were about to enter the land of Israel, the Jordan river also let us pass. When we received the Torah; all of nature celebrated. The mountains skipped like rams, and the hills like young lambs.

It was as if a voice called out to creation: O' sea, why do you split? O' Jordan, why do you turn back? Mountains, why do you skip like rams; hills like young lambs? And creation sings back it's answer: The earth is in awe of it's Creator; before the God of Jacob; The One who turns the rock into a pond of water, the flint into a flowing fountain.

43-47
P.S.K.

לְפִיכָךְ אֲנַחְנוּ חַיָּבִים לְהוֹדוֹת, לְהַלֵּל, לְשַׁבֵּחַ, לְפָאֵר, לְרוֹמֵם, לְהַדֵּר, לְבָרֵךְ, לְעַלֵּה וּלְקַלֵּס. לְמִי שֶׁעָשָׂה לַאֲבוֹתֵינוּ וְלָנוּ אֶת־כָּל־הַנִּסִּים הָאֵלּוּ. הוֹצִיאָנוּ מֵעַבְדוּת לְחֵרוּת. מִיָּגוֹן לְשִׂמְחָה. וּמֵאֵבֶל לְיוֹם טוֹב. וּמֵאֲפֵלָה לְאוֹר גָּדוֹל. וּמִשִּׁעְבּוּד לִגְאֻלָּה. וְנֹאמַר לְפָנָיו שִׁירָה חֲדָשָׁה הַלְלוּיָהּ:

הַלְלוּיָהּ הַלְלוּ עַבְדֵי יְהוָה, הַלְלוּ אֶת־שֵׁם יְהוָה: יְהִי שֵׁם יְהוָה מְבֹרָךְ מֵעַתָּה וְעַד־עוֹלָם: מִמִּזְרַח־שֶׁמֶשׁ עַד־מְבוֹאוֹ מְהֻלָּל שֵׁם יְהוָה: רָם עַל־כָּל־גּוֹיִם יְהוָה, עַל־הַשָּׁמַיִם כְּבוֹדוֹ: מִי כַּיהוָה אֱלֹהֵינוּ הַמַּגְבִּיהִי לָשָׁבֶת: הַמַּשְׁפִּילִי לִרְאוֹת בַּשָּׁמַיִם וּבָאָרֶץ: מְקִימִי מֵעָפָר דָּל, מֵאַשְׁפֹּת יָרִים אֶבְיוֹן: לְהוֹשִׁיבִי עִם־נְדִיבִים, עִם נְדִיבֵי עַמּוֹ: מוֹשִׁיבִי עֲקֶרֶת הַבַּיִת אֵם־הַבָּנִים שְׂמֵחָה הַלְלוּיָהּ:

בְּצֵאת יִשְׂרָאֵל מִמִּצְרָיִם, בֵּית יַעֲקֹב מֵעַם לֹעֵז: הָיְתָה יְהוּדָה לְקָדְשׁוֹ יִשְׂרָאֵל מַמְשְׁלוֹתָיו: הַיָּם רָאָה וַיָּנֹס, הַיַּרְדֵּן יִסֹּב לְאָחוֹר: הֶהָרִים רָקְדוּ כְאֵילִים גְּבָעוֹת כִּבְנֵי־צֹאן: מַה־לְּךָ הַיָּם כִּי תָנוּס, הַיַּרְדֵּן תִּסֹּב לְאָחוֹר: הֶהָרִים תִּרְקְדוּ כְאֵילִים גְּבָעוֹת כִּבְנֵי־צֹאן: מִלִּפְנֵי אָדוֹן חוּלִי אָרֶץ, מִלִּפְנֵי אֱלוֹהַּ יַעֲקֹב: הַהֹפְכִי הַצּוּר אֲגַם־מָיִם, חַלָּמִישׁ לְמַעְיְנוֹ־מָיִם:

HE LOWERS HIMSELF TO LOOK AT THE HEAVEN AND THE EARTH

The "heaven and the earth," are the spiritual and the physical. The lofty and the commonplace.

God is not an elitist who keeps company only with the upper-crust of the spiritually attuned, or who will only be seen at the most select of venues. God considers every aspect of every life to be of supreme value; from the most sublime moments of meditation and prayer, to the mundanity of eating and conjugal intimacy. Thus, in the eyes of a Jew, all moments are but vessels of potential waiting to be filled with value, with spirituality, and with meaning.

Next stop, grape juice and matzah.

Great, let's go!

Now that we have completed the final portion of the Haggadah text, we are ready to move on to some very important mitzvot, to the meal, and then to the conclusion of the seder.

At this point everyone should have a full cup of wine or grape juice in front of them. We will now drink the second of the four cups. The cup is lifted and the matzah is covered during the recitation of this blessing.

Blessed are You, Adonai our God, King of the universe, Who redeemed us and redeemed our ancestors from Egypt, and allowed us to arrive at this night so that we could eat matzah and maror. Therefore, Adonai, our God and God of our forefathers, enable us to experience future holidays and festivals in peace; joyful in the rebuilding of Your city, and happy in Your service. There we will eat of the many offerings, and of the Passover Offerings, whose blood will be upon the sides of Your altar and be acceptable. In your honor we will compose a new song that celebrates our redemption and our spiritual liberation. Blessed are You, Adonai, Who has redeemed Israel.

Blessed are You, Adonai, our God, King of the universe, Who creates the fruit of the vine.

בָּרוּךְ אַתָּה יְהֹוָה אֱלֹהֵינוּ מֶלֶךְ הָעוֹלָם, בּוֹרֵא פְּרִי הַגָּפֶן:

Baruch attah Adonai, eloheynu melech ha–olam, boray p'ri ha–gafen.

After the blessing, everyone drinks the second cup of wine. 1) Be careful not to speak after the blessing until the cup has been drunk. 2) Lean to the left while drinking. 3) Try to drink the entire cup, or at least most of it.

בָּרוּךְ אַתָּה יְהֹוָה אֱלֹהֵינוּ מֶלֶךְ הָעוֹלָם, אֲשֶׁר גְּאָלָנוּ וְגָאַל אֶת־אֲבוֹתֵינוּ מִמִּצְרַיִם, וְהִגִּיעָנוּ הַלַּיְלָה הַזֶּה לֶאֱכָל־בּוֹ מַצָּה וּמָרוֹר. כֵּן יְהֹוָה אֱלֹהֵינוּ וֵאלֹהֵי אֲבוֹתֵינוּ, יַגִּיעֵנוּ לְמוֹעֲדִים וְלִרְגָלִים אֲחֵרִים הַבָּאִים לִקְרָאתֵנוּ לְשָׁלוֹם, שְׂמֵחִים בְּבִנְיַן עִירֶךָ וְשָׂשִׂים בַּעֲבוֹדָתֶךָ, וְנֹאכַל שָׁם מִן הַזְּבָחִים וּמִן הַפְּסָחִים (בְּמוֹצָאֵי שַׁבָּת: מִן הַפְּסָחִים וּמִן הַזְּבָחִים) אֲשֶׁר יַגִּיעַ דָּמָם עַל קִיר מִזְבַּחֲךָ לְרָצוֹן, וְנוֹדֶה לְךָ שִׁיר חָדָשׁ עַל גְּאֻלָּתֵנוּ וְעַל פְּדוּת נַפְשֵׁנוּ: בָּרוּךְ אַתָּה יְהֹוָה גָּאַל יִשְׂרָאֵל:

בָּרוּךְ אַתָּה יְהֹוָה אֱלֹהֵינוּ מֶלֶךְ הָעוֹלָם, בּוֹרֵא פְּרִי הַגָּפֶן:

65
ƤＳＫ

RACHTZAH (WASHING THE HANDS)

The procedure for washing is identical to the washing done earlier at Urechatz. However, this washing will be followed by two blessings, and one should try not to speak from the time of the blessing until after eating the matzah. Everyone except the leader of the seder goes to the kitchen. A large cup is filled with water which is poured twice on the right hand and twice on the left. The Rachtzah blessing is recited, hands are dried, and everyone returns to the table to recite the next two blessings before eating the matzah. When possible, the leader of the seder should wash at the table.

Blessed are You, Adonai, our God, King of the universe, Who has sanctified us with His commandments, and commanded us with the washing of the hands.

בָּרוּךְ אַתָּה יְהֹוָה אֱלֹהֵינוּ מֶלֶךְ הָעוֹלָם, אֲשֶׁר קִדְּשָׁנוּ בְּמִצְוֹתָיו וְצִוָּנוּ עַל נְטִילַת יָדָיִם.

Baruch attah Adonai, eloheynu melech ha–olam, asher kid-shanu b'mitzvo-tav, ve–tzivanu al ne–tilat yada–yim.

66
ƤＳＫ

MOTZI (BLESSING FOR MATZAH)

At this point we fulfill the mitzvah to eat matzah on the night of Passover. Each person should have two–thirds of a piece of matzah on their plate; half a piece is sufficient if hand baked matzah is used.

The leader of the seder lifts all three matzahs from the seder plate and recites the following blessing.

Blessed are You, Adonai, our God, King of the universe, Who brings forth bread from the ground.

בָּרוּךְ אַתָּה יְהֹוָה אֱלֹהֵינוּ מֶלֶךְ הָעוֹלָם, הַמּוֹצִיא לֶחֶם מִן הָאָרֶץ:

Baruch attah Adonai, eloheynu melech ha–olam, ha–motzi lechem min ha–aretz.

The bottom matzah is put down, and the following blessing is recited while the top (whole) matzah, and the middle (broken) piece are still raised.

68-71
PSK

MATZAH

The bottom matzah is placed back on the seder plate before reciting the next blessing. Following this blessing, everyone should eat their piece of matzah while reclining on the left side. One should keep in mind that this blessing also relates to the korech–sandwich and the afikomen that will be eaten later.

Blessed are You, Adonai, our God, King of the universe, Who has sanctified us with his commandments, and has commanded us with the eating of matzah.

בָּרוּךְ אַתָּה יְהֹוָה אֱלֹהֵינוּ מֶלֶךְ הָעוֹלָם, אֲשֶׁר קִדְּשָׁנוּ בְּמִצְוֹתָיו וְצִוָּנוּ עַל אֲכִילַת מַצָּה:

Baruch attah Adonai, eloheynu melech ha–olam, asher kid–shanu b'mitzvo–tav, ve–tzivanu al achilat matzah.

MAROR (BITTER HERBS)

The leader of the seder dips a large piece of maror into charoset, and then shakes off the charoset. One such piece is given to each person. The following blessing also relates to the maror eaten with the korech–sandwich. After reciting the blessing, everyone eats the maror without reclining.

Blessed are You, Adonai, our God, King of the universe, Who has sanctified us with his commandments, and commanded us with the eating of maror.

בָּרוּךְ אַתָּה יְהֹוָה אֱלֹהֵינוּ מֶלֶךְ הָעוֹלָם, אֲשֶׁר קִדְּשָׁנוּ בְּמִצְוֹתָיו וְצִוָּנוּ עַל אֲכִילַת מָרוֹר:

Baruch attah Adonai, eloheynu melech ha–olam, asher kid–shanu b'mitzvo–tav, ve–tzivanu al achilat maror.

KORECH (SANDWICH)

The korech–sandwich is made as follows: Using one–third of a piece of matzah, and a large piece of maror that is dipped in charoset (the charoset is shaken off), one makes a sandwich that is eaten while reclining to the left. The following paragraph is said before one eats the matzah.

As a remembrance of the way we ate in the days of the Temple, we now do as the sage Hillel did. He would combine the Passover Offering, matzah, and maror in a sandwich and eat them together. This is a fulfillment of what it says in the Torah; "They shall eat it (the Passover Offering) with matzahs and bitter herbs."

כֵּן עָשָׂה הִלֵּל בִּזְמַן שֶׁבֵּית הַמִּקְדָּשׁ הָיָה קַיָּם. הָיָה כּוֹרֵךְ פֶּסַח מַצָּה וּמָרוֹר וְאוֹכֵל בְּיַחַד. כְּמוֹ שֶׁנֶּאֱמַר עַל מַצּוֹת וּמְרוֹרִים יֹאכְלֻהוּ:

SHULCHAN ORECH (THE FESTIVE MEAL)

Finally, what everyone has been waiting for! The festive Passover meal. While one should enjoy the Passover dinner, it is important to leave room for the afikomen.

TZAFON (AFIKOMEN)

Using the afikomen, and additional matzah as needed, each person receives two–thirds of a piece of matzah: half a piece is sufficient if hand–baked matzah is used. The afikomen should be eaten while leaning to the left.

BARECH (BLESSING AFTER DINNER)

Birkat Hamazon (the blessing after meals), is a special blessing said after a meal that included bread or matzah. Now that we have finished a delicious meal and enjoyed the seder together, we express our gratitude to God. Birkat Hamazon expresses an overwhelming sense of gratitude. At the same time that we are thankful for the blessing of food, our hearts overflow and we give thanks for Jerusalem and our homeland, Israel; for the Torah and for the privilege of being a Jew and a part of a nation with a unique relationship to God.

At this time, before Birkat Hamazon, the third cup of wine is poured. It is customary for people to fill one another's cup.

The hebrew Birkat Hamazon can be found on page 82. The concluding portions of the seder are found on page 85, following the hebrew Birkat Hamazon.

BIRKAT HAMAZON

Blessed are You, Adonai, our God, King of the universe, Who nourishes the whole world; in His goodness, with favor, with loving–kindness, and with compassion. He gives sustenance to all flesh, for His loving–kindness is eternal. And because of His great goodness we have never lacked food, and may it never be lacking to us forever. For the sake of His Great Name, because He is the God Who nourishes and sustains all beings, and does good to all of them, and He prepares food for all of His creatures which He has created. Blessed are You, Adonai, Who provides food for all.

We thank You, Adonai, our God, because You have given to our forefathers as a heritage; a desirable, good and spacious land; because You brought us forth, Adonai, our God, from the land of Egypt and You delivered us from the house of bondage; for Your covenant which You sealed in our flesh; and for Your Torah which You taught us, and for Your statutes which You made known to us; for life, favor, and loving–kindness which You granted us; and for the food with which You feed and sustain us constantly, every day, in every season, and in every hour.

For all this, Adonai, our God, we thank You and bless You. May Your Name be blessed continuously and forever by the

mouth of all living things. As it is written, 'And you shall eat and be satisfied and bless Adonai, your God, for the good land that He gave you.' Blessed are You, Adonai, for the land and for the food.

Have compassion Adonai, our God, on Israel Your people, on Jerusalem Your city, on Zion the resting place of Your Glory, on the kingdom of the house of David, Your anointed, and on the great and holy House upon which Your Name is proclaimed. Our God, our father—tend us, feed us, sustain us, nourish us, relieve us; Adonai, our God, grant us speedy relief from all our troubles. Please, Adonai, our God, let us not be needful of the gifts of human hands, nor of their loans—but only of Your Hand; that is full, open, holy, and generous; that we not feel shame or humiliation—forever and ever.

On the Sabbath add the following paragraph.

May it please You, Adonai, our God—fortify us through Your commandments and through the commandment relating to the seventh day, this great and holy Shabbat. For this day is great and holy before You, to observe the Shabbat on it, and to rest on it in love, as commanded by Your will. May it be Your will, Adonai, our God, that there be no distress, no grief, or sighing on this day of our rest. And show us, Adonai, our God, the consolation of Zion, Your city, and the rebuilding of Jerusalem, city of Your holiness, for You are the Master of salvations and Master of consolations.

Our God and God of our fathers, may there arise, come, reach, appear, be accepted, be heard, be counted, and be remembered before You—the remembrance of ourselves, the remembrance of our fathers; the remembrance of the Messiah, the son of David, Your servant; the remembrance of Jerusalem, Your holy city; and the remembrance of Your entire people, the House of Israel, before you. For survival, for well-being, for favor, for loving-kindness, and for compassion, for life and for peace on this day of the Festival of Matzos. Remember us on it, Adonai, our God, for goodness, count us on it for blessing, and deliver us on it for life. Regarding salvation and compassion, have pity, show favor and be compassionate upon us and help us. For our eyes are turned to You; for You are the Almighty King, gracious, and merciful.

Rebuild Jerusalem, the Holy City, speedily in our days. Blessed are You, Adonai, Who rebuilds Jerusalem. Amen.

Blessed are You, Adonai our God, King of the universe, the Almighty, our Father, our King, our Mighty One, our Creator, our Redeemer, our Maker, our Holy One, Holy One of Jacob; our Shepherd, the Shepherd of Israel, the king who is good and beneficent to all beings. For every single day He did good, does good, and will do good to us. He has rewarded us, is rewarding us, and will forever reward us—with favor and with loving-kindness and with compassion, with relief, salvation, success, blessing, help, consolation, sustenance, maintenance, mercy, life, peace, and everything good; and of all good things may He never deprive us.

The compassionate One. May He reign over us forever. The compassionate One. May He be blessed on heaven and on earth. The compassionate One. May He be praised for all generations, may He be glorified through us to all eternity, and be honored through us forever and ever. The compassionate One. May He sustain us in honor. The compassionate One. May He break the yoke of oppression from our necks and guide us upright to our land. The compassionate One. May He send us abundant blessing to this house and upon this table at which we have eaten. The compassionate One. May He send us Elijah the Prophet, who is remembered for good, to proclaim to us good tidings, salvations, and consolations. The compassionate One. May He bless—

Children at their parents' home add the words in parentheses:
**(my father, my teacher) the master of this house,
and (my mother, my teacher) lady of this house,**

Those eating at their own home recite the following, and add
the appropriate words in parentheses:
me, (my wife/husband and family) and all that is mine,

Guests recite the following:
them, their house, their family, and all that is theirs,

all continue here:
ours and all that is ours—just as our forefathers, Abraham, Isaac, and Jacob were blessed in everything, from everything,

with everything. So may He bless us all together with a perfect blessing. And let us say: Amen.

On high, may merit be invoked upon them and upon us, for the merit of peace. May we receive a blessing from Adonai and kindness from the God of our deliverance, and find favor and understanding in the eyes of God and man.

On the Sabbath add the following sentence:

The compassionate One. May He allow us to inherit the day which will be completely Shabbat, and rest for eternal life.

The words in parentheses are added on the two Seder nights:

The compassionate One. May He cause us to inherit that day which is totally good, (that eternal day, the day when the just will sit with crowns on their heads, enjoying their proximity to God—and may our portion be with them).

The compassionate One. May He make us worthy to experience the days of Messiah and the life of the World to Come. He Who is a tower of salvations to His King and shows loving-kindness to his anointed, to David and his descendants forever. He Who makes peace in His heavenly heights, may He make peace for us and for all Israel. And let us say: Amen.

Fear Adonai, His holy ones, for those who fear Him are not aware of deprivation. Young lions may feel want and hunger, but those who seek Adonai will not lack any good. Give thanks to God for He is good; His loving-kindness is eternal. You open Your hand and satisfy the desire of every living being. Blessed is the man who trusts in Adonai, and Adonai will be his trust. I was a youth and also have aged, and I have not seen a righteous man forsaken, with his children begging for bread. Adonai will give strength to His nation; Adonai will bless His nation with peace.

The following blessing is said before drinking the third cup of wine. One should try to finish the entire cup, or at least, most of it. Again, we are careful to lean to the left while drinking.

Blessed are You, Adonai, our God, King of the universe, Who creates the fruit of the vine.

בָּרוּךְ אַתָּה יְהֹוָה אֱלֹהֵינוּ מֶלֶךְ הָעוֹלָם, בּוֹרֵא פְּרִי הַגָּפֶן:

Baruch attah Adonai, eloheynu melech ha-olam, boray p'ri ha-gafen.

שִׁיר הַמַּעֲלוֹת בְּשׁוּב יְהוָה אֶת־שִׁיבַת צִיּוֹן הָיִינוּ כְּחֹלְמִים: אָז יִמָּלֵא שְׂחוֹק פִּינוּ וּלְשׁוֹנֵנוּ רִנָּה, אָז יֹאמְרוּ בַגּוֹיִם, הִגְדִּיל יְהוָה לַעֲשׂוֹת עִם־אֵלֶּה: הִגְדִּיל יְהוָה לַעֲשׂוֹת עִמָּנוּ הָיִינוּ שְׂמֵחִים: שׁוּבָה יְהוָה אֶת־שְׁבִיתֵנוּ כַּאֲפִיקִים בַּנֶּגֶב: הַזֹּרְעִים בְּדִמְעָה בְּרִנָּה יִקְצֹרוּ: הָלוֹךְ יֵלֵךְ וּבָכֹה נֹשֵׂא מֶשֶׁךְ־הַזָּרַע, בֹּא־יָבֹא בְרִנָּה נֹשֵׂא אֲלֻמֹּתָיו:

English continues on page 85.

בָּרוּךְ אַתָּה יְהוָה אֱלֹהֵינוּ מֶלֶךְ הָעוֹלָם, הַזָּן אֶת־הָעוֹלָם כֻּלּוֹ, בְּטוּבוֹ, בְּחֵן בְּחֶסֶד וּבְרַחֲמִים הוּא־נוֹתֵן לֶחֶם לְכָל־בָּשָׂר כִּי לְעוֹלָם חַסְדּוֹ: וּבְטוּבוֹ הַגָּדוֹל תָּמִיד לֹא־חָסַר לָנוּ וְאַל יֶחְסַר־לָנוּ מָזוֹן לְעוֹלָם וָעֶד: בַּעֲבוּר שְׁמוֹ הַגָּדוֹל כִּי הוּא אֵל זָן וּמְפַרְנֵס לַכֹּל, וּמֵטִיב לַכֹּל, וּמֵכִין מָזוֹן לְכָל־בְּרִיּוֹתָיו אֲשֶׁר בָּרָא, בָּרוּךְ אַתָּה יְהוָה הַזָּן אֶת־הַכֹּל:

נוֹדֶה לְךָ יְהוָה אֱלֹהֵינוּ עַל שֶׁהִנְחַלְתָּ לַאֲבוֹתֵינוּ אֶרֶץ חֶמְדָּה טוֹבָה וּרְחָבָה. וְעַל שֶׁהוֹצֵאתָנוּ יְהוָה אֱלֹהֵינוּ מֵאֶרֶץ מִצְרַיִם, וּפְדִיתָנוּ מִבֵּית עֲבָדִים, וְעַל־בְּרִיתְךָ שֶׁחָתַמְתָּ בִּבְשָׂרֵנוּ, וְעַל תּוֹרָתְךָ שֶׁלִּמַּדְתָּנוּ, וְעַל חֻקֶּיךָ שֶׁהוֹדַעְתָּנוּ וְעַל חַיִּים חֵן וָחֶסֶד שֶׁחוֹנַנְתָּנוּ וְעַל אֲכִילַת מָזוֹן שָׁאַתָּה זָן וּמְפַרְנֵס אוֹתָנוּ תָּמִיד, בְּכָל־יוֹם וּבְכָל־עֵת וּבְכָל־שָׁעָה:

וְעַל הַכֹּל יְהוָה אֱלֹהֵינוּ אֲנַחְנוּ מוֹדִים לָךְ, וּמְבָרְכִים אוֹתָךְ, יִתְבָּרַךְ שִׁמְךָ בְּפִי כָּל־חַי תָּמִיד לְעוֹלָם וָעֶד: כַּכָּתוּב, וְאָכַלְתָּ וְשָׂבָעְתָּ, וּבֵרַכְתָּ אֶת־יְהוָה אֱלֹהֶיךָ עַל־הָאָרֶץ הַטֹּבָה אֲשֶׁר נָתַן־לָךְ: בָּרוּךְ אַתָּה יְהוָה, עַל־הָאָרֶץ, וְעַל־הַמָּזוֹן:

רַחֵם יְהוָה אֱלֹהֵינוּ עַל־יִשְׂרָאֵל עַמֶּךָ, וְעַל־יְרוּשָׁלַיִם עִירֶךָ, וְעַל צִיּוֹן מִשְׁכַּן כְּבוֹדֶךָ, וְעַל מַלְכוּת בֵּית דָּוִד מְשִׁיחֶךָ, וְעַל־הַבַּיִת הַגָּדוֹל וְהַקָּדוֹשׁ שֶׁנִּקְרָא שִׁמְךָ עָלָיו: אֱלֹהֵינוּ אָבִינוּ רוֹעֵנוּ זוֹנֵנוּ פַּרְנְסֵנוּ וְכַלְכְּלֵנוּ וְהַרְוִיחֵנוּ, וְהַרְוַח לָנוּ יְהוָה אֱלֹהֵינוּ מְהֵרָה מִכָּל־צָרוֹתֵינוּ: וְנָא אַל תַּצְרִיכֵנוּ יְהוָה אֱלֹהֵינוּ, לֹא לִידֵי מַתְּנַת בָּשָׂר וָדָם, וְלֹא לִידֵי הַלְוָאָתָם, כִּי אִם לְיָדְךָ הַמְּלֵאָה הַפְּתוּחָה הַקְּדוֹשָׁה וְהָרְחָבָה, שֶׁלֹּא נֵבוֹשׁ וְלֹא נִכָּלֵם לְעוֹלָם וָעֶד:

בשבת :

רְצֵה וְהַחֲלִיצֵנוּ יְהוָה אֱלֹהֵינוּ בְּמִצְוֹתֶיךָ, וּבְמִצְוַת יוֹם הַשְּׁבִיעִי הַשַּׁבָּת הַגָּדוֹל וְהַקָּדוֹשׁ הַזֶּה, כִּי יוֹם זֶה גָּדוֹל וְקָדוֹשׁ הוּא לְפָנֶיךָ, לִשְׁבָּת־בּוֹ וְלָנוּחַ־בּוֹ בְּאַהֲבָה כְּמִצְוַת רְצוֹנֶךָ, וּבִרְצוֹנְךָ הָנִיחַ לָנוּ יְהוָה אֱלֹהֵינוּ, שֶׁלֹּא תְהֵא צָרָה וְיָגוֹן וַאֲנָחָה בְּיוֹם מְנוּחָתֵנוּ. וְהַרְאֵנוּ יְהוָה אֱלֹהֵינוּ בְּנֶחָמַת צִיּוֹן עִירֶךָ, וּבְבִנְיַן יְרוּשָׁלַיִם עִיר קָדְשֶׁךָ, כִּי אַתָּה הוּא בַּעַל הַיְשׁוּעוֹת וּבַעַל הַנֶּחָמוֹת:

אֱלֹהֵינוּ וֵאלֹהֵי אֲבוֹתֵינוּ, יַעֲלֶה, וְיָבֹא, וְיַגִּיעַ, וְיֵרָאֶה, וְיֵרָצֶה, וְיִשָּׁמַע, וְיִפָּקֵד, וְיִזָּכֵר, זִכְרוֹנֵנוּ וּפִקְדוֹנֵנוּ. וְזִכְרוֹן אֲבוֹתֵינוּ, וְזִכְרוֹן מָשִׁיחַ בֶּן־דָּוִד עַבְדֶּךָ. וְזִכְרוֹן יְרוּשָׁלַיִם עִיר קָדְשֶׁךָ. וְזִכְרוֹן כָּל־עַמְּךָ בֵּית יִשְׂרָאֵל לְפָנֶיךָ, לִפְלֵיטָה לְטוֹבָה, לְחֵן וּלְחֶסֶד וּלְרַחֲמִים, וּלְחַיִּים טוֹבִים וּלְשָׁלוֹם. בְּיוֹם חַג הַמַּצּוֹת הַזֶּה. זָכְרֵנוּ יְהוָה אֱלֹהֵינוּ בּוֹ לְטוֹבָה, וּפָקְדֵנוּ בוֹ לִבְרָכָה, וְהוֹשִׁיעֵנוּ בוֹ לְחַיִּים טוֹבִים: וּבִדְבַר יְשׁוּעָה וְרַחֲמִים חוּס וְחָנֵּנוּ וְרַחֵם עָלֵינוּ וְהוֹשִׁיעֵנוּ, כִּי אֵלֶיךָ עֵינֵינוּ, כִּי אֵל מֶלֶךְ חַנּוּן וְרַחוּם אָתָּה:

וּבְנֵה יְרוּשָׁלַיִם עִיר הַקֹּדֶשׁ בִּמְהֵרָה בְיָמֵינוּ. בָּרוּךְ אַתָּה יְהֹוָה, בֹּנֵה בְרַחֲמָיו יְרוּשָׁלָיִם. אָמֵן:

בָּרוּךְ אַתָּה יְהֹוָה אֱלֹהֵינוּ מֶלֶךְ הָעוֹלָם, הָאֵל אָבִינוּ מַלְכֵּנוּ אַדִּירֵנוּ בּוֹרְאֵנוּ גֹּאֲלֵנוּ יוֹצְרֵנוּ קְדוֹשֵׁנוּ קְדוֹשׁ יַעֲקֹב, רוֹעֵנוּ רוֹעֵה יִשְׂרָאֵל, הַמֶּלֶךְ הַטּוֹב וְהַמֵּטִיב לַכֹּל, שֶׁבְּכָל יוֹם וָיוֹם הוּא הֵיטִיב לָנוּ. הוּא מֵטִיב לָנוּ. הוּא יֵיטִיב לָנוּ. הוּא גְמָלָנוּ הוּא גוֹמְלֵנוּ הוּא יִגְמְלֵנוּ לָעַד, לְחֵן וּלְחֶסֶד וּלְרַחֲמִים, וּלְרֶוַח הַצָּלָה וְהַצְלָחָה, בְּרָכָה וִישׁוּעָה. נֶחָמָה פַּרְנָסָה וְכַלְכָּלָה וְרַחֲמִים וְחַיִּים וְשָׁלוֹם וְכָל־ טוֹב, וּמִכָּל טוּב לְעוֹלָם אַל יְחַסְּרֵנוּ:

הָרַחֲמָן הוּא יִמְלוֹךְ עָלֵינוּ לְעוֹלָם וָעֶד:

הָרַחֲמָן הוּא יִתְבָּרֵךְ בַּשָּׁמַיִם וּבָאָרֶץ:

הָרַחֲמָן הוּא יִשְׁתַּבַּח לְדוֹר דּוֹרִים, וְיִתְפָּאַר בָּנוּ לָעַד וּלְנֵצַח נְצָחִים, וְיִתְהַדַּר בָּנוּ לָעַד וּלְעוֹלְמֵי עוֹלָמִים:

הָרַחֲמָן הוּא יְפַרְנְסֵנוּ בְּכָבוֹד:

הָרַחֲמָן הוּא יִשְׁבּוֹר עֻלֵּנוּ מֵעַל צַוָּארֵנוּ וְהוּא יוֹלִיכֵנוּ קוֹמְמִיּוּת לְאַרְצֵנוּ:

הָרַחֲמָן הוּא יִשְׁלַח, בְּרָכָה מְרֻבָּה בְּבַיִת זֶה, וְעַל שֻׁלְחָן זֶה שֶׁאָכַלְנוּ עָלָיו:

הָרַחֲמָן הוּא יִשְׁלַח לָנוּ אֶת־אֵלִיָּהוּ הַנָּבִיא זָכוּר לַטּוֹב, וִיבַשֶּׂר־לָנוּ בְּשׂוֹרוֹת טוֹבוֹת יְשׁוּעוֹת וְנֶחָמוֹת:

הָרַחֲמָן הוּא יְבָרֵךְ אֶת־אָבִי מוֹרִי בַּעַל הַבַּיִת הַזֶּה, וְאֶת־אִמִּי מוֹרָתִי בַּעֲלַת הַבַּיִת הַזֶּה, אוֹתָם וְאֶת־בֵּיתָם וְאֶת־זַרְעָם וְאֶת־כָּל־אֲשֶׁר לָהֶם, אוֹתָנוּ וְאֶת־כָּל־ אֲשֶׁר לָנוּ: כְּמוֹ שֶׁנִּתְבָּרְכוּ־אֲבוֹתֵינוּ אַבְרָהָם, יִצְחָק, וְיַעֲקֹב בַּכֹּל מִכֹּל כֹּל, כֵּן יְבָרֵךְ אוֹתָנוּ כֻּלָּנוּ יַחַד בִּבְרָכָה שְׁלֵמָה וְנֹאמַר אָמֵן:

בַּמָּרוֹם יְלַמְּדוּ עָלֵינוּ זְכוּת שֶׁתְּהֵא לְמִשְׁמֶרֶת שָׁלוֹם. וְנִשָּׂא בְרָכָה מֵאֵת יְהֹוָה, וּצְדָקָה מֵאֱלֹהֵי יִשְׁעֵנוּ, וְנִמְצָא חֵן וְשֵׂכֶל טוֹב בְּעֵינֵי אֱלֹהִים וְאָדָם:

בשבת:

הָרַחֲמָן הוּא יַנְחִילֵנוּ יוֹם שֶׁכֻּלוֹ שַׁבָּת וּמְנוּחָה לְחַיֵּי הָעוֹלָמִים:

ביום טוב:

הָרַחֲמָן הוּא יַנְחִילֵנוּ יוֹם שֶׁכֻּלוֹ טוֹב:

הָרַחֲמָן הוּא יְזַכֵּנוּ לִימוֹת הַמָּשִׁיחַ וּלְחַיֵּי הָעוֹלָם הַבָּא. מִגְדֹּל יְשׁוּעוֹת מַלְכּוֹ וְעֹשֶׂה חֶסֶד לִמְשִׁיחוֹ לְדָוִד וּלְזַרְעוֹ עַד עוֹלָם: עֹשֶׂה שָׁלוֹם בִּמְרוֹמָיו, הוּא יַעֲשֶׂה שָׁלוֹם עָלֵינוּ וְעַל כָּל יִשְׂרָאֵל, וְאִמְרוּ אָמֵן:

יְראוּ אֶת־יְהֹוָה קְדֹשָׁיו כִּי־אֵין מַחְסוֹר לִירֵאָיו: כְּפִירִים רָשׁוּ וְרָעֵבוּ וְדֹרְשֵׁי יְהֹוָה לֹא־יַחְסְרוּ כָל־טוֹב: הוֹדוּ לַיהֹוָה כִּי־טוֹב, כִּי לְעוֹלָם חַסְדּוֹ: פּוֹתֵחַ אֶת־יָדֶךָ וּמַשְׂבִּיעַ לְכָל חַי רָצוֹן: בָּרוּךְ הַגֶּבֶר אֲשֶׁר יִבְטַח בַּיהֹוָה וְהָיָה יְהֹוָה מִבְטַחוֹ: נַעַר הָיִיתִי גַּם זָקַנְתִּי, וְלֹא רָאִיתִי צַדִּיק נֶעֱזָב, וְזַרְעוֹ מְבַקֶּשׁ לָחֶם. יְהֹוָה עֹז לְעַמּוֹ יִתֵּן, יְהֹוָה יְבָרֵךְ אֶת עַמּוֹ בַשָּׁלוֹם.

וּמְבָרֵךְ עַל הַכּוֹס וְשׁוֹתָה בַּהֲסִיבָה:

בָּרוּךְ אַתָּה יְהֹוָה אֱלֹהֵינוּ מֶלֶךְ הָעוֹלָם בּוֹרֵא פְּרִי הַגָּפֶן:

In case anyone is leaving or going to sleep now, we want to thank all of you for inviting us to your seder. It was a pleasure meeting you and we hope you enjoyed the seder. For those of you who are hanging in there, don't forget—there are still some beautiful blessings to say, and one more cup of wine to drink.

30
אסך

The fourth cup of wine is now poured. Also, the Cup of Elijah (Eliyahu the Prophet) is poured at this point.

The front door to the house is now opened. This is in keeping with the idea that the night of Passover is considered *laiyl shimurim*, "a night of guarded protection." With the door open, the following paragraph is recited.

We're over here.

God, pour Your anger on the nations that refuse to pay attention to You, and that insist on defining good and evil in a way that suits their needs; and on the kingdoms that do not take Your existence into consideration. It is nations like these that have tried to annihilate the Jewish people; that destroyed our Temple, and that drove us from our land. Pour Your anger upon them, and let Your wrath finally catch–up to them. Pursue them with wrath and annihilate them from the beautiful world You created; the world that they destroy, the world that You created.

שְׁפֹךְ חֲמָתְךָ אֶל־הַגּוֹיִם אֲשֶׁר לֹא יְדָעוּךָ. וְעַל מַמְלָכוֹת אֲשֶׁר בְּשִׁמְךָ לֹא קָרָאוּ: כִּי אָכַל אֶת־יַעֲקֹב וְאֶת־נָוֵהוּ הֵשַׁמּוּ: שְׁפָךְ־עֲלֵיהֶם זַעְמֶךָ, וַחֲרוֹן אַפְּךָ יַשִּׂיגֵם: תִּרְדֹּף בְּאַף וְתַשְׁמִידֵם מִתַּחַת שְׁמֵי יְהוָה:

HALLEL (PRAISE)

After closing the door, everyone recites the Hallel–Praises. These should be read at a comfortable pace. The seder concludes on page 91 and the Hebrew Hallel is on page 94.

HALLEL

Not for our sake, O God, not for our sake; but for Your Name's sake give honor, for the sake of Your loving–kindness and Your truth. Why should the nations say: 'Where is their God?' Our God is in the heavens; everything is according to His will. Their idols are silver and gold, the work of human hands. They have a mouth, but cannot speak; they have eyes, but cannot see; they have ears, but cannot hear; they have a nose, but cannot smell; their hands–cannot touch; their feet–cannot walk; nor can they utter a sound with their throat. Those who make them should become like them, whoever trusts in them. O' Israel. Trust in Adonai–He is their help and shield! House of Aaron. Trust in Adonai. He is their help and shield. You who fear Adonai. Trust in Adonai, He is their help and shield.

Adonai, Who has remembered us; will bless. He will bless the House of Israel; He will bless the House of Aaron; He will bless those who fear Adonai, the small and also the great. May Adonai add increase upon you, upon you and your children! You are blessed of Adonai, who makes the heaven and earth. The heaven: the heaven is Adonai's; but the earth: He has given to mankind. The dead cannot praise Adonai, nor any who go down in silence. But we will bless our God from this time forward, forever. Halleluyah!

I love when Adonai hears my voice, my prayers. For He has inclined His ear to me, throughout my days I will call upon Him. The pangs of death encompassed me; the narrow confines of the grave have caught–up with me; trouble and sorrow I have found. Then I called upon the Name of Adonai: 'Please Adonai, save my soul.' Gracious is Adonai and righteous, our God is merciful. God protects the simple; I was brought low, and He saved me. Return my soul to your rest, for Adonai has greatly rewarded you. You freed my soul from death, my eyes from tears, and my foot from stumbling. I will walk before God in the lands of the living. I kept faith although I say: 'I suffer very much.' I said in my haste: 'All mankind is deceitful.'
How can I repay Adonai for all the favors He has given me? I will raise the cup of deliverance, and call in the Name of Adonai. My vows to Adonai will I fulfill in the presence of his entire people. Precious in the eyes of Adonai is the death of His devoted ones. Please, Adonai, for I am Your servant, I am Your servant, son of Your handmaid. You have released my bonds. To You I sacrifice thanksgiving offerings, and the Name of Adonai will I invoke. My vows to Adonai will I fulfill in the presence of His entire people; in the courtyards of the House of Adonai, in your midst, Jerusalem. Halleluyah!
Praise Adonai, all you nations; praise Him, all you peoples! For His kindness to us was overwhelming, and the truth of Adonai is eternal. Halleluyah!

Give thanks to Adonai for he is good; His kindness endures forever!

Let Israel say: His kindness endures forever!

Let the House of Aaron Say: His kindness endures forever!

Let them who fear Adonai say: His kindness endures forever!

From out of the straits I called to God; God answered me with a feeling of expansiveness. Adonai is with me, and so I do not fear; what can man do to me? Adonai is with me, to help me; therefore I can face my enemies. It is better to rely on Adonai than to rely on princes. All nations surround me; but in the Name of Adonai I cut them down. They surround me. They surrounded me from all sides; but in the Name of Adonai, I cut them down. They surround me like bees, but they are extinguished like the thorns by fire; in the Name of Adonai I cut them down. You have continuously pushed me that I might fall, but Adonai assisted me. My strength and song is God; He has become my salvation. The sound of rejoicing and salvation is in the tents of the righteous: The right hand of Adonai does valiantly! The right hand of Adonai is raised triumphantly! The right hand of Adonai is exalted. I shall not die! I shall live and relate the deeds of God. God has chastised me exceedingly, but He did not let me die. Open for me the gates of righteousness, I will enter them and be thankful to God. This is the gate of Adonai; the righteous shall enter through it. I thank You for You answered me and became my deliverance. I thank You for You answered me and became my deliverance. The very stone which the builders despised has become the cornerstone. The very stone which the builders despised has become the corner–stone. This was done by Adonai; it is wondrous in our eyes. This was done by Adonai; it is wondrous in our eyes. This is the day Adonai has made; we will rejoice and be happy in Him. This is the day Adonai has made; we will rejoice and be happy in Him.

Adonai, please save us!

Adonai, please save us!

Adonai, please make us prosper!

Adonai, please make us prosper!

Blessed is the one who comes in the Name of Adonai; we bless you from the House of Adonai. Blessed is the one who comes in the Name of Adonai; we bless you from the House of thank You; my God, I will exalt You. You are my God and I will thank you, my God, I will exalt You. Be grateful to Adonai, for He is good; His kindness endures forever. Be grateful to Adonai, for He is good; His kindness endures forever.

They will praise You, Adonai our God, for all of Your deeds; along with Your devoted followers, the righteous, who do Your will, and Your entire nation, the House of Israel; joyfully thank you, bless, praise, laud, exalt, revere, sanctify, and crown Your name, our King. For to You it is proper to give thanks, and to Your name it is appropriate to sing praises, for from eternity and to eternity You are God. Blessed are You God, the One who is most praiseworthy.

Give thanks to Adonai, for He is good;
His kindness endures forever!
Give thanks to the God of gods; His kindness endures forever!
Give thanks to the Master of masters; His kindness endures forever!
To the only one who does great wonders; His kindness endures forever!
To He who fashioned the cosmos with understanding;
His kindness endures forever!
To Him Who placed the earth over the waters;
His kindness endures forever!
To Him Who made the great celestial lights;
His kindness endures forever!
The sun to reign during day; His kindness endures forever!
The moon and the stars to reign at night;
His kindness endures forever!
To Him Who struck the Egyptians through their firstborn;
His kindness endures forever!
And removed Israel from amongst them;
His kindness endures forever!
With a strong hand and an outstretched arm;
His kindness endures forever!
He Who divided the Sea into parts; His kindness endures forever!
And caused Israel to pass through it; His kindness endures forever!
And threw Pharaoh and his army into the Sea of Reeds;

His kindness endures forever!
To Him Who led His people through the wilderness;
His kindness endures forever!
To Him Who destroyed great kings;His kindness endures forever!
And slew mighty kings;His kindness endures forever!
Sichon, king of Emorites;His kindness endures forever!
And Og, king of Bashan;His kindness endures forever!
And gave their land as an inheritance; His kindness endures forever!
An inheritance of Israel. His servant:His kindness endures forever!
He Who remembered us at our lowest moment;
His kindness endures forever!
And released us from our enemies;His kindness endures forever!
He gives food to all living creatures;His kindness endures forever!
Be thankful to God of heaven;His kindness endures forever!

The soul of every living being will bless Your Name, Adonai our God; All spirited flesh will continuously glorify and exalt Your remembrance, our King. From eternity to eternity, You are God, and besides You we have no king, redeemer or helper. O Rescuer, Redeemer, Sustainer and Merciful One in all times of desperation and distress. We have no King but You – God of the first and of the last, God of all creatures, Master of all genera-tions, Who is extolled through numerous praises, He Who guides His world with kindness and His creatures with compas-sion Adonai does not slumber or sleep; He rouses the sleepers and awakens the ones who slumber; He makes the mute speak and frees those who are imprisoned; He supports the ones who are falling and raises erect the bowed down. Only to you do we give thanks.

If our mouths were as full of song as the sea, and our tongue as full of rejoicing as its many waves, and our lips as full of praise as the expanse of the heavens, and our eyes as brilliant as the sun and the moon, and our hands as outspread in prayer as the eagles of the sky and our feet as swift as deer: Still we could not thank You enough. Adonai our God and God of our fathers, bless Your Name, for each one of the thousands and thousands and myriads upon myriads of kindness, miracles and wonders, which You performed for our fathers, and for us. You liberated us from Egypt. Adonai our God, and took us out of the house of bondage. In famine You nourished us, and in plenty You were the source of our support. You saved us from the sword, from the plague You let us escape; and You spared us from severe and enduring diseases. Until now Your compassion has helped us, and Your kindness has never left us. Do not abandon us, Adonai our God—never.

The limbs that You set within us, and the spirit and soul that You breathed into our nostrils, and the tongue that You put in our mouth – they must all thank and bless, praise and glorify, exalt, be devoted to, sanctify and honor Your Name, our King, forever. Every mouth must give thanks to You, every tongue must vow allegiance to You; every knee must bend to You; all who stand must bow before You; all hearts must fear You; and men's innermost feelings and thoughts will certainly sing praises to Your name, as it is written; All my bones will say: 'Adonai, who is like You?' You save the poor man from the one who is stronger than him, the impoverished and the needy from one who would try to rob him. Who can be compared to You? Who is equal to You? Who can be compared to You? Great, powerful, and awesome God, supreme God, Maker of heaven and earth. We shall praise, extol, and glorify You; and bless Your holy Name, as it says; A Psalm of David: Bless Adonai, my soul, and let my whole being bless His holy name.

God, in the omnipotence of Your strength, great is the honor of Your name, externally powerful and awesome through Your wondrous deeds, King who is enthroned on a high and lofty throne.

He Who abides eternally, exalted and holy is His Name. And it is written: Be joyful in Adonai, you righteous ones; for the upright, His praise is fitting. By the mouth of the upright You will be praised; by the words of the righteous You will be blessed; by the tongue of the devoted You will be exalted; and amongst the holy You will be sanctified.

And in the assemblies of Your countless people, the House of Israel, with excitement will Your name, our King, be glorified

in every generation. For such is the responsibility of all creatures; before You, Adonai, our God and God of our fathers, to
thank, praise, laud, glorify, extol, adore, bless, exalt, and sing
praises; even beyond all expressions of the songs and praises of
David the son of Jesse, Your servant, Your anointed one.

May Your Name be praised forever, our King, the God and
King Who is great and holy in heaven and on earth; for to You,
Adonai our God and God of our fathers, it is most fitting to sing
song and praise, hallel and hymns, strength and sovereignty,
victory, greatness and power; praise and glory, holiness and
sovereignty, blessing and thanks; from now and forever. Blessed
are You, Adonai, God, King, who is praised greatly, God of
thanksgiving, Master of wonders, Who favors songs of
praise–King, God, Life of all worlds.

27
PSK

At the conclusion of Hallel, the fourth cup of wine is drunk. One should
finish all or most of the cup. As with the other cups, one leans to the left while
drinking. The following blessing is said before one begins to drink.

**Blessed are You, Adonai, our God, King of the universe, Who
creates the fruit of the vine.**

בָּרוּךְ אַתָּה יְהֹוָה אֱלֹהֵינוּ מֶלֶךְ הָעוֹלָם, בּוֹרֵא פְּרִי הַגָּפֶן:

**Baruch attah Adonai, eloheynu melech ha–olam, boray p'ri
ha–gafen.**

The following blessing is recited after drinking the fourth cup. The phrases
in parentheses are added on the Sabbath.

**Blessed are You, Adonai, our God, King of the universe, for
the vine and the fruit of the vine; and for the produce of the
field: For the lovely, good, and spacious land that You graciously
gave our forefathers as an inheritance: To eat its fruit and be
filled by its goodness. Please have compassion, Adonai, our God,
on Israel Your nation, on Jerusalem Your city, and on Zion
where Your honor dwells; and on Your altar and on Your
Temple. May You rebuild Jerusalem, Your holy city, quickly in
our days: And take us up to it and let us rejoice in its rebuilding,
and let us eat from its fruit and be filled with its goodness: And
bless You in a state of sanctity and purity. (Find favor with us
and give us strength on this Shabbat day.) And let us be happy**

on this Festival of Matzahs. **You, Adonai, are good and benevo–lent to all creatures, and we give thanks to You for the land and the fruit of the vine. Blessed are You, Adonai, for the land and the fruit of the vine.**

בָּרוּךְ אַתָּה יְהֹוָה אֱלֹהֵינוּ מֶלֶךְ הָעוֹלָם, עַל הַגֶּפֶן וְעַל פְּרִי הַגֶּפֶן וְעַל תְּנוּבַת הַשָּׂדֶה, וְעַל־אֶרֶץ חֶמְדָּה טוֹבָה וּרְחָבָה, שֶׁרָצִיתָ וְהִנְחַלְתָּ לַאֲבוֹתֵינוּ לֶאֱכֹל מִפִּרְיָהּ וְלִשְׂבּוֹעַ מִטּוּבָהּ. רַחֶם נָא יְהֹוָה אֱלֹהֵינוּ עַל־יִשְׂרָאֵל עַמֶּךָ, וְעַל־יְרוּשָׁלַם עִירֶךָ, וְעַל־צִיּוֹן מִשְׁכַּן כְּבוֹדֶךָ, וְעַל־מִזְבְּחֶךָ וְעַל־הֵיכָלֶךָ. וּבְנֵה יְרוּשָׁלַם עִיר הַקֹּדֶשׁ בִּמְהֵרָה בְיָמֵינוּ וְהַעֲלֵנוּ לְתוֹכָהּ. וְשַׂמְּחֵנוּ בְּבִנְיָנָהּ וְנֹאכַל מִפִּרְיָהּ וְנִשְׂבַּע מִטּוּבָהּ וּנְבָרֶכְךָ בִּקְדֻשָּׁה וּבְטָהֳרָה. (בשבת: וּרְצֵה וְהַחֲלִיצֵנוּ בְּיוֹם הַשַּׁבָּת הַזֶּה:) וְזָכְרֵנוּ לְטוֹבָה בְּיוֹם חַג הַמַּצּוֹת הַזֶּה. כִּי אַתָּה יְהֹוָה טוֹב וּמֵטִיב לַכֹּל, וְנוֹדֶה לְּךָ עַל הָאָרֶץ וְעַל פְּרִי הַגֶּפֶן: בָּרוּךְ אַתָּה יְהֹוָה עַל הָאָרֶץ וְעַל פְּרִי הַגֶּפֶן.

NIRTZAH

We have now reached the summit of our seder experience. Here, at the peak of our Passover celebration, we are joined by countless other Jewish families who celebrate Passover all over the world; and hundreds of generations of our people who have participated in seders ever since that very night when we were freed from Egypt.

It has truly been a privilege to spend this seder with you. We now join together: In our hearts we join with Jews everywhere, and in our souls with Jews throughout the ages; and together we invoke those words that unite us like no others–Next Year in Jerusalem.

The following prayer is read by everyone.

The Seder is now concluded in accordance with it's laws; it's observances, and all it's guidelines. Just as we have been blessed to experience this seder, so may we be privileged to experience every aspect of the seder in the Temple in Jerusalem.

O' God who is the transcendent source of all spirituality, please enable the Jewish nation to fulfill it's potential; it's mission. Please guide us, we who feel our Jewishness to be a blessing; and quickly bring us to Zion; and let our hearts overflow with excitement, with joy and with song.

L'SHANA HABAH B'YERUSHOLAYIM – NEXT YEAR IN JERUSALEM !

חֲסַל סִדּוּר פֶּסַח כְּהִלְכָתוֹ, כְּכָל מִשְׁפָּטוֹ וְחֻקָּתוֹ, כַּאֲשֶׁר זָכִינוּ לְסַדֵּר אוֹתוֹ, כֵּן נִזְכֶּה לַעֲשׂוֹתוֹ. זָךְ שׁוֹכֵן מְעוֹנָה, קוֹמֵם קְהַל עֲדַת מִי מָנָה, בְּקָרוֹב נַהֵל נִטְעֵי כַנָּה, פְּדוּיִם לְצִיּוֹן בְּרִנָּה.

לְשָׁנָה הַבָּאָה בִּירוּשָׁלָיִם:

NEXT YEAR IN JERUSALEM

Every synagogue in the world faces Jerusalem. In prayer—no matter where we are—our hearts are directed towards Jerusalem. As the *ne'ilah* service draws to a close at the conclusion of Yom Kippur, congregations the world over proclaim, "Next year in Jerusalem." At a wedding, the groom breaks a glass under the chuppah, and for a moment, all thoughts are on Jerusalem. And again tonight. In the waning moments of the seder, every Jewish family prays—*Next year in Jerusalem.*

The word Jerusalem means, "city of peace." Peace, *shalom*, is not merely the absence of conflict. Peace is the seamless harmony of individuals genuinely embracing a common vision. Not that each becomes lost in some faceless wave of the masses, but that each aspires to lend the beauty of his or her being to the realization of a dream.

With Nirtzah, we lift our vision to the city of peace; to the imminence of Jerusalem: The imminence of peace.

Jerusalem embodies our inner calling, our destiny. That the wisdom and way of Jewish life should work to liberate the potential of every Jew, of the Jewish nation, and thus to transform the landscape of history. That somehow the intimate relationship of one small people to God should bear the fruits of universal spiritual symphony.

The fruit of freedom is peace. Peace of mind. Peace of body and soul. Peace within us, and so too, between us.

לֹא לָנוּ יְהֹוָה לֹא לָנוּ כִּי לְשִׁמְךָ תֵּן כָּבוֹד עַל־חַסְדְּךָ עַל־אֲמִתֶּךָ: לָמָּה
יֹאמְרוּ הַגּוֹיִם אַיֵּה־נָא אֱלֹהֵיהֶם: וֵאלֹהֵינוּ בַשָּׁמָיִם כֹּל אֲשֶׁר־חָפֵץ עָשָׂה:
עֲצַבֵּיהֶם כֶּסֶף וְזָהָב מַעֲשֵׂה יְדֵי אָדָם: פֶּה־לָהֶם וְלֹא יְדַבֵּרוּ עֵינַיִם לָהֶם וְלֹא יִרְאוּ:
אָזְנַיִם לָהֶם וְלֹא יִשְׁמָעוּ אַף לָהֶם וְלֹא יְרִיחוּן: יְדֵיהֶם וְלֹא יְמִישׁוּן רַגְלֵיהֶם וְלֹא
יְהַלֵּכוּ לֹא־יֶהְגּוּ בִּגְרוֹנָם: כְּמוֹהֶם יִהְיוּ עֹשֵׂיהֶם כֹּל אֲשֶׁר־בֹּטֵחַ בָּהֶם: יִשְׂרָאֵל
בְּטַח בַּיהֹוָה עֶזְרָם וּמָגִנָּם הוּא: בֵּית אַהֲרֹן בִּטְחוּ בַיהֹוָה עֶזְרָם וּמָגִנָּם הוּא: יִרְאֵי
יְהֹוָה בִּטְחוּ בַיהֹוָה עֶזְרָם וּמָגִנָּם הוּא:
יְהֹוָה זְכָרָנוּ יְבָרֵךְ, יְבָרֵךְ אֶת־בֵּית יִשְׂרָאֵל, יְבָרֵךְ אֶת־בֵּית אַהֲרֹן: יְבָרֵךְ יִרְאֵי
יְהֹוָה, הַקְּטַנִּים עִם־הַגְּדֹלִים: יֹסֵף יְהֹוָה עֲלֵיכֶם, עֲלֵיכֶם וְעַל־בְּנֵיכֶם: בְּרוּכִים
אַתֶּם לַיהֹוָה עֹשֵׂה שָׁמַיִם וָאָרֶץ: הַשָּׁמַיִם שָׁמַיִם לַיהֹוָה וְהָאָרֶץ נָתַן לִבְנֵי־אָדָם:
לֹא־הַמֵּתִים יְהַלְלוּ־יָהּ וְלֹא כָּל־יֹרְדֵי דוּמָה: וַאֲנַחְנוּ נְבָרֵךְ יָהּ מֵעַתָּה וְעַד־עוֹלָם
הַלְלוּיָהּ:

אָהַבְתִּי כִּי־יִשְׁמַע יְהֹוָה אֶת־קוֹלִי תַּחֲנוּנָי: כִּי־הִטָּה אָזְנוֹ לִי וּבְיָמַי אֶקְרָא:
אֲפָפוּנִי חֶבְלֵי־מָוֶת וּמְצָרֵי שְׁאוֹל מְצָאוּנִי צָרָה וְיָגוֹן אֶמְצָא: וּבְשֵׁם־יְהֹוָה אֶקְרָא
אָנָּה יְהֹוָה מַלְּטָה נַפְשִׁי: חַנּוּן יְהֹוָה וְצַדִּיק וֵאלֹהֵינוּ מְרַחֵם: שֹׁמֵר פְּתָאִים יְהֹוָה
דַּלּוֹתִי וְלִי יְהוֹשִׁיעַ: שׁוּבִי נַפְשִׁי לִמְנוּחָיְכִי כִּי־יְהֹוָה גָּמַל עָלָיְכִי: כִּי חִלַּצְתָּ נַפְשִׁי
מִמָּוֶת אֶת־עֵינִי מִן־דִּמְעָה אֶת־רַגְלִי מִדֶּחִי: אֶתְהַלֵּךְ לִפְנֵי יְהֹוָה בְּאַרְצוֹת
הַחַיִּים: הֶאֱמַנְתִּי כִּי אֲדַבֵּר אֲנִי עָנִיתִי מְאֹד: אֲנִי אָמַרְתִּי בְחָפְזִי כָּל־הָאָדָם כֹּזֵב:
מָה־אָשִׁיב לַיהֹוָה כָּל־תַּגְמוּלוֹהִי עָלָי: כּוֹס־יְשׁוּעוֹת אֶשָּׂא וּבְשֵׁם יְהֹוָה
אֶקְרָא: נְדָרַי לַיהֹוָה אֲשַׁלֵּם נֶגְדָה־נָּא לְכָל־עַמּוֹ: יָקָר בְּעֵינֵי יְהֹוָה הַמָּוְתָה
לַחֲסִידָיו: אָנָּה יְהֹוָה כִּי־אֲנִי עַבְדֶּךָ אֲנִי עַבְדְּךָ בֶּן־אֲמָתֶךָ פִּתַּחְתָּ לְמוֹסֵרָי: לְךָ
אֶזְבַּח זֶבַח תּוֹדָה וּבְשֵׁם יְהֹוָה אֶקְרָא: נְדָרַי לַיהֹוָה אֲשַׁלֵּם נֶגְדָה־נָּא לְכָל־עַמּוֹ:
בְּחַצְרוֹת בֵּית יְהֹוָה בְּתוֹכֵכִי יְרוּשָׁלִָם הַלְלוּיָהּ:
הַלְלוּ אֶת־יְהֹוָה כָּל־גּוֹיִם שַׁבְּחוּהוּ כָּל־הָאֻמִּים: כִּי גָבַר עָלֵינוּ חַסְדּוֹ וֶאֱמֶת־
יְהֹוָה לְעוֹלָם הַלְלוּיָהּ:

הוֹדוּ לַיהֹוָה כִּי־טוֹב, כִּי לְעוֹלָם חַסְדּוֹ:
יֹאמַר־נָא יִשְׂרָאֵל, כִּי לְעוֹלָם חַסְדּוֹ:
יֹאמְרוּ נָא בֵית־אַהֲרֹן, כִּי לְעוֹלָם חַסְדּוֹ:
יֹאמְרוּ נָא יִרְאֵי יְהֹוָה, כִּי לְעוֹלָם חַסְדּוֹ:

מִן־הַמֵּצַר קָרָאתִי יָּהּ עָנָנִי בַמֶּרְחָב יָהּ: יְהֹוָה לִי לֹא אִירָא, מַה־יַּעֲשֶׂה לִי
אָדָם: יְהֹוָה לִי בְּעֹזְרָי וַאֲנִי אֶרְאֶה בְשֹׂנְאָי: טוֹב לַחֲסוֹת בַּיהֹוָה מִבְּטֹחַ בָּאָדָם:
טוֹב לַחֲסוֹת בַּיהֹוָה מִבְּטֹחַ בִּנְדִיבִים: כָּל־גּוֹיִם סְבָבוּנִי בְּשֵׁם יְהֹוָה כִּי אֲמִילַם:
סַבּוּנִי גַם־סְבָבוּנִי בְּשֵׁם יְהֹוָה כִּי אֲמִילַם: סַבּוּנִי כִדְבֹרִים דֹּעֲכוּ כְּאֵשׁ קוֹצִים
בְּשֵׁם יְהֹוָה כִּי אֲמִילַם: דָּחֹה דְחִיתַנִי לִנְפֹּל, וַיהֹוָה עֲזָרָנִי: עָזִּי וְזִמְרָת יָהּ וַיְהִי־לִי
לִישׁוּעָה: קוֹל רִנָּה וִישׁוּעָה בְּאָהֳלֵי צַדִּיקִים, יְמִין יְהֹוָה עֹשָׂה חָיִל: יְמִין יְהֹוָה
רוֹמֵמָה, יְמִין יְהֹוָה עֹשָׂה חָיִל: לֹא־אָמוּת כִּי־אֶחְיֶה, וַאֲסַפֵּר מַעֲשֵׂי־יָהּ: יַסֹּר יִסְּרַנִּי
יָּהּ, וְלַמָּוֶת לֹא נְתָנָנִי: פִּתְחוּ־לִי שַׁעֲרֵי־צֶדֶק אָבֹא־בָם אוֹדֶה יָהּ: זֶה־הַשַּׁעַר
לַיהֹוָה צַדִּיקִים יָבֹאוּ בוֹ: אוֹדְךָ כִּי עֲנִיתָנִי וַתְּהִי־לִי לִישׁוּעָה: אוֹדְךָ כִּי עֲנִיתָנִי
וַתְּהִי־לִי לִישׁוּעָה: אֶבֶן מָאֲסוּ הַבּוֹנִים הָיְתָה לְרֹאשׁ פִּנָּה: אֶבֶן מָאֲסוּ הַבּוֹנִים
הָיְתָה לְרֹאשׁ פִּנָּה: מֵאֵת יְהֹוָה הָיְתָה זֹּאת הִיא נִפְלָאת בְּעֵינֵינוּ: מֵאֵת יְהֹוָה
הָיְתָה זֹּאת הִיא נִפְלָאת בְּעֵינֵינוּ: זֶה־הַיּוֹם עָשָׂה יְהֹוָה נָגִילָה וְנִשְׂמְחָה בוֹ: זֶה־
הַיּוֹם עָשָׂה יְהֹוָה נָגִילָה וְנִשְׂמְחָה בוֹ:

אָנָּא יְהֹוָה הוֹשִׁיעָה נָּא: אָנָּא יְהֹוָה הוֹשִׁיעָה נָּא:

אָנָּא יְהֹוָה הַצְלִיחָה נָּא: אָנָּא יְהֹוָה הַצְלִיחָה נָּא:

בָּרוּךְ הַבָּא בְּשֵׁם יְהֹוָה בֵּרַכְנוּכֶם מִבֵּית יְהֹוָה: בָּרוּךְ הַבָּא בְּשֵׁם יְהֹוָה בֵּרַכְנוּכֶם מִבֵּית יְהֹוָה: אֵל יְהֹוָה וַיָּאֶר לָנוּ אִסְרוּ־חַג בַּעֲבֹתִים עַד קַרְנוֹת הַמִּזְבֵּחַ: אֵל יְהֹוָה וַיָּאֶר לָנוּ אִסְרוּ־חַג בַּעֲבֹתִים עַד קַרְנוֹת הַמִּזְבֵּחַ: אֵלִי אַתָּה וְאוֹדֶךָּ אֱלֹהַי אֲרוֹמְמֶךָּ: אֵלִי אַתָּה וְאוֹדֶךָּ אֱלֹהַי אֲרוֹמְמֶךָּ: הוֹדוּ לַיהֹוָה כִּי־טוֹב כִּי לְעוֹלָם חַסְדּוֹ: הוֹדוּ לַיהֹוָה כִּי־טוֹב כִּי לְעוֹלָם חַסְדּוֹ:

יְהַלְלוּךָ יְהֹוָה אֱלֹהֵינוּ כָּל־מַעֲשֶׂיךָ וַחֲסִידֶיךָ צַדִּיקִים עוֹשֵׂי רְצוֹנֶךָ, וְכָל־עַמְּךָ בֵּית יִשְׂרָאֵל בְּרִנָּה יוֹדוּ וִיבָרְכוּ וִישַׁבְּחוּ וִיפָאֲרוּ וִירוֹמְמוּ וְיַעֲרִיצוּ וְיַקְדִּישׁוּ וְיַמְלִיכוּ אֶת־שִׁמְךָ מַלְכֵּנוּ. כִּי לְךָ טוֹב לְהוֹדוֹת וּלְשִׁמְךָ נָאֶה לְזַמֵּר, כִּי מֵעוֹלָם וְעַד עוֹלָם אַתָּה אֵל:

הוֹדוּ לַיהֹוָה כִּי־טוֹב, כִּי לְעוֹלָם חַסְדּוֹ:

הוֹדוּ לֵאלֹהֵי הָאֱלֹהִים, כִּי לְעוֹלָם חַסְדּוֹ:

הוֹדוּ לַאֲדֹנֵי הָאֲדֹנִים, כִּי לְעוֹלָם חַסְדּוֹ:

לְעֹשֵׂה נִפְלָאוֹת גְּדֹלוֹת לְבַדּוֹ, כִּי לְעוֹלָם חַסְדּוֹ:

לְעֹשֵׂה הַשָּׁמַיִם בִּתְבוּנָה, כִּי לְעוֹלָם חַסְדּוֹ:

לְרוֹקַע הָאָרֶץ עַל־הַמָּיִם, כִּי לְעוֹלָם חַסְדּוֹ:

לְעֹשֵׂה אוֹרִים גְּדֹלִים, כִּי לְעוֹלָם חַסְדּוֹ:

אֶת־הַשֶּׁמֶשׁ לְמֶמְשֶׁלֶת בַּיּוֹם, כִּי לְעוֹלָם חַסְדּוֹ:

אֶת־הַיָּרֵחַ וְכוֹכָבִים לְמֶמְשְׁלוֹת בַּלַּיְלָה, כִּי לְעוֹלָם חַסְדּוֹ:

לְמַכֵּה מִצְרַיִם בִּבְכוֹרֵיהֶם, כִּי לְעוֹלָם חַסְדּוֹ:

וַיּוֹצֵא יִשְׂרָאֵל מִתּוֹכָם, כִּי לְעוֹלָם חַסְדּוֹ:

בְּיָד חֲזָקָה וּבִזְרוֹעַ נְטוּיָה, כִּי לְעוֹלָם חַסְדּוֹ:

לְגֹזֵר יַם־סוּף לִגְזָרִים, כִּי לְעוֹלָם חַסְדּוֹ:

וְהֶעֱבִיר יִשְׂרָאֵל בְּתוֹכוֹ, כִּי לְעוֹלָם חַסְדּוֹ:

וְנִעֵר פַּרְעֹה וְחֵילוֹ בְיַם־סוּף, כִּי לְעוֹלָם חַסְדּוֹ:

לְמוֹלִיךְ עַמּוֹ בַּמִּדְבָּר, כִּי לְעוֹלָם חַסְדּוֹ:

לְמַכֵּה מְלָכִים גְּדֹלִים, כִּי לְעוֹלָם חַסְדּוֹ:

וַיַּהֲרֹג מְלָכִים אַדִּירִים, כִּי לְעוֹלָם חַסְדּוֹ:

לְסִיחוֹן מֶלֶךְ הָאֱמֹרִי, כִּי לְעוֹלָם חַסְדּוֹ:

וּלְעוֹג מֶלֶךְ הַבָּשָׁן, כִּי לְעוֹלָם חַסְדּוֹ:

וְנָתַן אַרְצָם לְנַחֲלָה, כִּי לְעוֹלָם חַסְדּוֹ:

נַחֲלָה לְיִשְׂרָאֵל עַבְדּוֹ, כִּי לְעוֹלָם חַסְדּוֹ:

שֶׁבְּשִׁפְלֵנוּ זָכַר לָנוּ, כִּי לְעוֹלָם חַסְדּוֹ:

וַיִּפְרְקֵנוּ מִצָּרֵינוּ, כִּי לְעוֹלָם חַסְדּוֹ:

נוֹתֵן לֶחֶם לְכָל־בָּשָׂר, כִּי לְעוֹלָם חַסְדּוֹ:

הוֹדוּ לְאֵל הַשָּׁמָיִם, כִּי לְעוֹלָם חַסְדּוֹ:

נִשְׁמַת כָּל חַי תְּבָרֵךְ אֶת שִׁמְךָ יהוה אֱלֹהֵינוּ, וְרוּחַ כָּל בָּשָׂר תְּפָאֵר וּתְרוֹמֵם
זִכְרְךָ מַלְכֵּנוּ תָּמִיד: מִן הָעוֹלָם וְעַד הָעוֹלָם אַתָּה אֵל, וּמִבַּלְעָדֶיךָ אֵין לָנוּ מֶלֶךְ
גּוֹאֵל וּמוֹשִׁיעַ: פּוֹדֶה וּמַצִּיל וּמְפַרְנֵס וּמְרַחֵם בְּכָל עֵת צָרָה וְצוּקָה. אֵין לָנוּ מֶלֶךְ
אֶלָּא אָתָּה: אֱלֹהֵי הָרִאשׁוֹנִים וְהָאַחֲרוֹנִים, אֱלוֹהַּ כָּל בְּרִיּוֹת, אֲדוֹן כָּל תּוֹלָדוֹת,
הַמְּהֻלָּל בְּרֹב הַתִּשְׁבָּחוֹת. הַמְּנַהֵג עוֹלָמוֹ בְּחֶסֶד וּבְרִיּוֹתָיו בְּרַחֲמִים: יהוה לֹא
יָנוּם וְלֹא יִישָׁן. הַמְּעוֹרֵר יְשֵׁנִים וְהַמֵּקִיץ נִרְדָּמִים וְהַמֵּשִׂיחַ אִלְּמִים וְהַמַּתִּיר
אֲסוּרִים, וְהַסּוֹמֵךְ נוֹפְלִים וְהַזּוֹקֵף כְּפוּפִים, לְךָ לְבַדְּךָ אֲנַחְנוּ מוֹדִים. אִלּוּ פִינוּ
מָלֵא שִׁירָה כַיָּם, וּלְשׁוֹנֵנוּ רִנָּה כַּהֲמוֹן גַּלָּיו, וְשִׂפְתוֹתֵינוּ שֶׁבַח כְּמֶרְחֲבֵי רָקִיעַ,
וְעֵינֵינוּ מְאִירוֹת כַּשֶּׁמֶשׁ וְכַיָּרֵחַ, וְיָדֵינוּ פְרוּשׂוֹת כְּנִשְׁרֵי שָׁמָיִם, וְרַגְלֵינוּ קַלּוֹת
כָּאַיָּלוֹת: אֵין אֲנַחְנוּ מַסְפִּיקִים לְהוֹדוֹת לְךָ, יהוה אֱלֹהֵינוּ וֵאלֹהֵי אֲבוֹתֵינוּ,
וּלְבָרֵךְ אֶת שְׁמֶךָ, עַל אַחַת מֵאֶלֶף אַלְפֵי אֲלָפִים וְרִבֵּי רְבָבוֹת פְּעָמִים הַטּוֹבוֹת,
שֶׁעָשִׂיתָ עִם אֲבוֹתֵינוּ וְעִמָּנוּ. מִלְּפָנִים מִמִּצְרַיִם גְּאַלְתָּנוּ, יהוה אֱלֹהֵינוּ, וּמִבֵּית
עֲבָדִים פְּדִיתָנוּ, בְּרָעָב זַנְתָּנוּ, וּבְשָׂבָע כִּלְכַּלְתָּנוּ, מֵחֶרֶב הִצַּלְתָּנוּ וּמִדֶּבֶר
מִלַּטְתָּנוּ, וּמֵחֳלָאִים רָעִים וְנֶאֱמָנִים דִּלִּיתָנוּ: עַד הֵנָּה עֲזָרוּנוּ רַחֲמֶיךָ, וְלֹא עֲזָבוּנוּ
חֲסָדֶיךָ. וְאַל תִּטְּשֵׁנוּ יְיָ אֱלֹהֵינוּ לָנֶצַח. עַל כֵּן אֵבָרִים שֶׁפִּלַּגְתָּ בָּנוּ, וְרוּחַ וּנְשָׁמָה
שֶׁנָּפַחְתָּ בְּאַפֵּנוּ, וְלָשׁוֹן אֲשֶׁר שַׂמְתָּ בְּפִינוּ, הֵן הֵם יוֹדוּ וִיבָרְכוּ וִישַׁבְּחוּ וִיפָאֲרוּ
וִישׁוֹרְרוּ וִירוֹמְמוּ וְיַעֲרִיצוּ וְיַקְדִּישׁוּ וְיַמְלִיכוּ אֶת שִׁמְךָ מַלְכֵּנוּ. כִּי כָל פֶּה לְךָ יוֹדֶה,
וְכָל לָשׁוֹן לְךָ תְּשָׁבַע, וְכָל בֶּרֶךְ לְךָ תִכְרַע, וְכָל קוֹמָה לְפָנֶיךָ תִשְׁתַּחֲוֶה: וְכָל
הַלְּבָבוֹת יִירָאוּךָ, וְכָל קֶרֶב וּכְלָיוֹת יְזַמְּרוּ לִשְׁמֶךָ, כַּדָּבָר שֶׁכָּתוּב: כָּל עַצְמוֹתַי
תֹּאמַרְנָה יהוה מִי כָמוֹךָ: מַצִּיל עָנִי מֵחָזָק מִמֶּנּוּ וְעָנִי וְאֶבְיוֹן מִגֹּזְלוֹ: מִי יִדְמֶה-
לָּךְ וּמִי יִשְׁוֶה-לָּךְ וּמִי יַעֲרָךְ-לָךְ, הָאֵל הַגָּדוֹל הַגִּבּוֹר וְהַנּוֹרָא, אֵל עֶלְיוֹן קוֹנֵה
שָׁמַיִם וָאָרֶץ: נְהַלֶּלְךָ וּנְשַׁבֵּחֲךָ וּנְפָאֶרְךָ וּנְבָרֵךְ אֶת שֵׁם קָדְשֶׁךָ, כָּאָמוּר: לְדָוִד,
בָּרְכִי נַפְשִׁי אֶת יהוה וְכָל קְרָבַי אֶת שֵׁם קָדְשׁוֹ: הָאֵל בְּתַעֲצֻמוֹת עֻזֶּךָ, הַגָּדוֹל
בִּכְבוֹד שְׁמֶךָ, הַגִּבּוֹר לָנֶצַח, וְהַנּוֹרָא בְּנוֹרְאוֹתֶיךָ, הַמֶּלֶךְ הַיּוֹשֵׁב עַל כִּסֵּא רָם
וְנִשָּׂא:

שׁוֹכֵן עַד, מָרוֹם וְקָדוֹשׁ שְׁמוֹ. וְכָתוּב רַנְּנוּ צַדִּיקִים בַּיהוה לַיְשָׁרִים נָאוָה
תְהִלָּה: בְּפִי יְשָׁרִים תִּתְהַלָּל, וּבְשִׂפְתֵי צַדִּיקִים תִּתְבָּרַךְ, וּבִלְשׁוֹן חֲסִידִים
תִּתְרוֹמָם, וּבְקֶרֶב קְדוֹשִׁים תִּתְקַדָּשׁ:

וּבְמַקְהֲלוֹת רִבְבוֹת עַמְּךָ בֵּית יִשְׂרָאֵל בְּרִנָּה יִתְפָּאֵר שִׁמְךָ מַלְכֵּנוּ בְּכָל דּוֹר
וָדוֹר. שֶׁכֵּן חוֹבַת כָּל הַיְצוּרִים, לְפָנֶיךָ, יהוה אֱלֹהֵינוּ וֵאלֹהֵי אֲבוֹתֵינוּ, לְהוֹדוֹת
לְהַלֵּל לְשַׁבֵּחַ, לְפָאֵר לְרוֹמֵם לְהַדֵּר לְבָרֵךְ לְעַלֵּה וּלְקַלֵּס, עַל כָּל דִּבְרֵי שִׁירוֹת
וְתִשְׁבְּחוֹת דָּוִד בֶּן יִשַׁי עַבְדְּךָ מְשִׁיחֶךָ:

יִשְׁתַּבַּח שִׁמְךָ לָעַד, מַלְכֵּנוּ, הָאֵל הַמֶּלֶךְ הַגָּדוֹל וְהַקָּדוֹשׁ בַּשָּׁמַיִם וּבָאָרֶץ כִּי
לְךָ נָאֶה יהוה אֱלֹהֵינוּ וֵאלֹהֵי אֲבוֹתֵינוּ, שִׁיר וּשְׁבָחָה, הַלֵּל וְזִמְרָה, עֹז וּמֶמְשָׁלָה,
נֶצַח, גְּדֻלָּה וּגְבוּרָה, תְּהִלָּה וְתִפְאֶרֶת, קְדֻשָּׁה וּמַלְכוּת, בְּרָכוֹת וְהוֹדָאוֹת מֵעַתָּה
וְעַד עוֹלָם: בָּרוּךְ אַתָּה יהוה, אֵל מֶלֶךְ גָּדוֹל בַּתִּשְׁבָּחוֹת, אֵל הַהוֹדָאוֹת, אֲדוֹן
הַנִּפְלָאוֹת, הַבּוֹחֵר בְּשִׁירֵי זִמְרָה, מֶלֶךְ, אֵל, חַי הָעוֹלָמִים:

Fun Facts — The Answers

1) The word seder means "order," and the reason this word is used is because the seder needs to follow a certain order.
2) Reclining at the meal is a sign of wealth, royalty and freedom.
3) You should recline on your left. If you recline on your right, you run the risk of opening-up your wind pipe (trachea) and choking.
4) Abraham (Avraham), Isaac (Yitzchak), and Jacob (Yaacov).
5) Abraham had to spend some time in Egypt, though Jacob was the only patriarch who lived there for an extended period of time. Jacob lived in Egypt for a total of seventeen years.
6) Matzah reminds us of both slavery and freedom. Matzah reminds us of slavery because it is the food that we were fed when we were slaves: On the other hand, matzah reminds us of freedom because it is the type of bread that we baked on the way out of Egypt.
7) The Torah speaks of five types of grain and only these five can be used to make matzah: Wheat, spelt, barley, oats and rye.
8) The word Haggadah means, "to tell." The reason this word is used, is because the Torah tells us "to tell" our children about the experience of the Jewish people in Egypt.
9) Joseph.
10) Joseph was Jacob's favorite son and displayed the potential to be a great leader. Unfortunately, Joseph's brothers were jealous of him. As a result, they eventually sold Joseph to a caravan of spice merchants that were traveling to Egypt. In Egypt, Joseph was sold to a government minister where he eventually was put in charge of the minister's personal affairs.
11) Sarah (Sara), Rebecca (Rivka), Rachel and Leah.
12) Ten.
13) Berashit (Genesis), Shemot (Exodus), Vayikra (Leviticus), Bamidbar (Numbers) and Devarim (Deuteronomy.
14) **Berashit**—the lives of the patriarchs and matriarchs from the time of Abraham until Jacob and his family settled in Egypt. Extra Credit: Berashit also contains the story of creation, Adam

and Eve, Cain and Abel, the flood and Noah's Ark and the tower of Babel. **Shemot**—the story of slavery in Egypt and the redemption. This book also contains the giving of the Torah at Mt. Sinai. **Vayikra**—the laws that relate to all the activities that take place in the Temple in Jerusalem. **Bamidbar**—the story of the forty years that the Jewish people spent in the desert before entering the land of Israel. **Devarim**—the final speech and lessons that Moses delivered to the Jewish people shortly before he died and just before the Jews went into Israel under the leadership of Joshua.

15) Five.

16) 613. 365 negative and 248 positive.

17) Shavuot and Sukkot.

18) Joseph eventually became prime minister of Egypt and only Pharoah had more power than Joseph. Background: Joseph worked for an Egyptian minister named Potifar. As a result of a false accusation Joseph was thrown in jail. While in jail, Joseph gained a reputation for being able to interpret dreams. Eventually he was called on to interpret a disturbing dream that Pharaoh had. Joseph predicted that Egypt would experience seven years of plentiful harvests followed by seven years of famine. Pharoah was impressed by Joseph's ability and appointed him Prime Minister of Egypt.

19) The district of Goshen.

20) Two mitzvot from the Torah— 1) To eat matzah on the night of Passover, 2) To tell the story of being freed from Egypt. Three mitzvot instituted by the sages of the Talmud— 1) To drink four cups of wine or grape juice, 2) To eat maror, 3) To recite the hallel/praises.

21) The Sea of Reeds split to allow the Jewish people to escape the pursuit of the Egyptian army.

22) God gave the Torah to the Jewish people.

23) Shavuot.

24) The Torah uses four different words to describe the transition from slavery to freedom. 1) V'hotzati— "and I removed you" 2)V'hitzalti— "and I rescued you" 3) V'goalti— "and I redeemed you" 4) V'lakachti— "and I took you"

26) Blood, frogs, lice, invasion of wild animals, animal epidemic, lice, hail, locust, darkness, death of the first born.

27) Aaron, the brother of Moses.

28) There was a famine that affected Egypt as well as Israel. Egypt however, thanks to the leadership of Joseph, had stored up food during the seven years of bounty. Jacob's family went to Egypt to buy food and they were eventually reunited with their brother Joseph. The brother who they sold was now Prime Minister of Egypt and savior of his family.

29) Rosh Hashanah, Yom Kippur, Sukkot, Shemini Atzeret, Passover, Shavuot.

30) Chanukah, Purim, The Ninth of Av (Tisha B'av).

31) Joseph wanted to keep his family separate from the general Egyptian population. To achieve this, he made a point of telling Pharaoh that his brothers were shepherds. Since sheep were a primary Egyptian god, the Egyptians did not want to live near a people that did not revere their god. For this reason the Jews were given the district of Goshen.

32) The three matzahs represent the three types of Jews. Kohen, Levi and Yisroel.

33) To remind us of the mortar and bricks that the Jews had to make.

34) Yes. The mitzvah to tell about leaving Egypt applies even if there are only adults, and even if only one person is making a seder.

35) Trick question! Joseph is buried in Israel. When the Jewish people left Egypt they took the body of Joseph with them to bury in Israel.

36) Nobody knows.

37) Fooled you again! Jacob is buried with the other patriarchs and matriarchs in the city of Hebron. Before he died, Jacob asked his son Joseph, Prime Minister of Egypt, to make sure that he be buried in Hebron.

38) Seventy people.

39) To remind us of the Passover Offering that we eat in the time of the Temple.

40) Nisan.

41) Tishrei, Cheshvan, Kislev, Tevet, Shevat, Adar, (Adar II), Nisan, Iyar, Sivan, Tammuz, Av, Elul.

42) 210 years.

43) Not only did the Nile river turn to blood, but so did all other waters in Egypt. Also, if a Jew wanted water from the river he got water, but an Egyptian could only get blood. And even if an Egyptian took a glass of water from a Jew, it would turn to blood.

44) The hail stones were balls of ice with a fiery core.

45) When Moses was a baby his mother hid him in a basket that she placed in the Nile. The river played a part in saving the life of Moses. For this reason it was not proper for Moses to strike the river with a plague. This teaches an important lesson about gratitude: If we should be grateful to something like a river, than we should certainly be careful to be thankful when people do us a favor.

46) Even though the Egyptians were our enemies and were justly punished, we are still saddened that people had to suffer. The removal of wine shows that our rejoicing is slightly tempered by the knowledge that others are in pain.

47) The Jewish people received the Torah at Mt. Sinai.

48) Reclining is a sign of freedom and the maror reminds us of slavery, not freedom.

49) Three times. Once for the mitzvah of matzah, a second time when you eat the Hillel sandwich and a third time for the afikomen.

50) Tricked ya'! We do recline when we eat the matzah.

51) The Jewish people, under the leadership of Joshua, the greatest disciple of Moses, entered the promised land of Israel.

52) To sanctify the new month with the appearance of the new moon. Note: The Jewish calendar is a lunar, not a solar calendar.

53) Because it's delicious!

Songs For The End Of The Seder

I. AND IT HAPPENED AT MIDNIGHT

You performed many miracles; at night. They occurred at the beginning of; this night. You helped Abraham, the righteous convert, to defeat his enemies; at night. And it was at midnight.

You judged the king of Gerar in a dream; at night. You frightened Laban in darkness; at night. And Jacob was able to defeat the adversary; at night. And it was at midnight.

You destroyed the Egyptian firstborn; at midnight. They were unable to find their hidden treasure when they got up; that night You used the stars to vanquish the enemy; at night. And it was at midnight.

A siege was planned for Jerusalem, but you miraculously destroyed that army; at night. You brought down those who worshiped the infamous idol, Baal; at night. To Daniel you revealed the secret of the dream; at night. And it was at midnight.

The one who drank from the Temple vessels, was killed; at night. The righteous one who was saved from the lion's den, and interpreted dreams; at night. Haman, who wrote a decree against the Jews, was undone; at night. And it was at midnight.

The king could not sleep, and this began the enemies downfall; at night. The evil nations will be stamped out when the exile comes to an end; at night. In the end light will shine for the righteous, and there will be only darkness for the enemy; at night. And it was at midnight.

Hasten the day that will be full of light; and no night. Let it de clear that the day belongs only to You; and so the night. Let the day shine even; at night. And it was at midnight.

וּבְכֵן וַיְהִי בַּחֲצִי הַלַּיְלָה.

אָז רוֹב נִסִּים הִפְלֵאתָ   בַּלַּיְלָה.
בְּרֹאשׁ אַשְׁמוֹרֶת זֶה   הַלַּיְלָה.
גֵּר צֶדֶק נִצַּחְתּוֹ כְּנֶחֱלַק לוֹ   לַיְלָה.
וַיְהִי בַּחֲצִי הַלַּיְלָה:

דַּנְתָּ מֶלֶךְ גְּרָר בַּחֲלוֹם   הַלַּיְלָה.
הִפְחַדְתָּ אֲרַמִּי בְּאֶמֶשׁ   לַיְלָה.
וַיָּשַׂר יִשְׂרָאֵל לְמַלְאָךְ וַיּוּכַל לוֹ   לַיְלָה.
וַיְהִי בַּחֲצִי הַלַּיְלָה:

זֶרַע בְּכוֹרֵי פַתְרוֹס מָחַצְתָּ בַּחֲצִי   הַלַּיְלָה.
חֵילָם לֹא מָצְאוּ בְּקוּמָם   בַּלַּיְלָה.
טִיסַת נְגִיד חֲרֹשֶׁת סִלִּיתָ בְּכוֹכְבֵי   לַיְלָה.
וַיְהִי בַּחֲצִי הַלַּיְלָה:

יָעֵץ מְחָרֵף לְנוֹפֵף אִוּוּי הוֹבַשְׁתָּ פְגָרָיו | בַּלַּיְלָה.
כָּרַע בֵּל וּמַצָּבוֹ בְּאִישׁוֹן | לַיְלָה.
לְאִישׁ חֲמוּדוֹת נִגְלָה רָז חָזוֹת | לַיְלָה.
וַיְהִי בַּחֲצִי הַלַּיְלָה:

מִשְׁתַּכֵּר בִּכְלֵי קֹדֶשׁ נֶהֱרַג בּוֹ | בַּלַּיְלָה.
נוֹשַׁע מִבּוֹר אֲרָיוֹת פּוֹתֵר בִּעֲתוּתֵי | לַיְלָה.
שִׂנְאָה נָטַר אֲגָגִי וְכָתַב סְפָרִים | בַּלַּיְלָה.
וַיְהִי בַּחֲצִי הַלַּיְלָה:

עוֹרַרְתָּ נִצְחֲךָ עָלָיו בְּנֶדֶד שְׁנַת | בַּלַּיְלָה.
פּוּרָה תִדְרוֹךְ לְשׁוֹמֵר מַה | לַיְלָה.
צָרַח כַּשּׁוֹמֵר וְשָׂח אָתָא בוֹקֶר וְגַם | לַיְלָה.
וַיְהִי בַּחֲצִי הַלַּיְלָה:

קָרֵב יוֹם אֲשֶׁר הוּא לֹא יוֹם וְלֹא | לַיְלָה.
רָם הוֹדַע כִּי לְךָ הַיּוֹם אַף לְךָ | הַלַּיְלָה.
שׁוֹמְרִים הַפְקֵד לְעִירְךָ כָּל הַיּוֹם וְכָל | הַלַּיְלָה.
תָּאִיר כְּאוֹר יוֹם חֶשְׁכַּת | לַיְלָה.
וַיְהִי בַּחֲצִי הַלַּיְלָה:

II. And You Will Say; This is the Passover Offering

You have displayed your awesome power; on Passover. You gave it the status of the first of all the Festivals; Passover. You revealed to Abraham what would happen; on Passover. And you will say, "this is the Passover Offering."

You visited Abraham in the heat of the day; on Passover. He then fed his visitors matzah; on Passover. And he ran to the cattle; a symbol of the Festival offering; on Passover. And you will say, "this is the Passover Offering."

The evil inhabitants of Sodom were consumed by fire; on Passover. But Lot went his own way and made matzah; on Passover. You destroyed the cities of Moph and Noph; on Passover. And you will say, "this is the Passover Offering."

You killed the firstborn while we were protected; on Passover. You passed over the Jewish homes that had blood on the door posts; on Passover. You held off the Angel of Death; on Passover. And you will say, "this is the Passover Offering."

The strong walled city was conquered; on Passover. The merit of the Omer Offering saved us from Midian; on Passover. The Syrian warriors went down in fire; on Passover. And you will say, "this is the Passover Offering."

The general was poised to destroy Jerusalem; on Passover. The writing on the wall foretold the end; on Passover. The sentries watched for the coming attack, while the king sat at his table; on Passover. And you will say, "this is the Passover Offering."

Esther gathered the Jews for a three day fast; on Passover. Then

Haman was hung on the gallows; on Passover.   May even greater misfortune befall Edom; on Passover.   May you make your presence clear, as You did on that holy night; Passover.   And you will say, "this is the Passover Offering."

וּבְכֵן וַאֲמַרְתֶּם זֶבַח פֶּסַח

אֹמֶץ גְּבוּרוֹתֶיךָ הִפְלֵאתָ בַּפֶּסַח.
בְּרֹאשׁ כָּל מוֹעֲדוֹת נִשֵּׂאתָ פֶּסַח.
גִּלִּיתָ לְאֶזְרָחִי חֲצוֹת לֵיל פֶּסַח.
וַאֲמַרְתֶּם זֶבַח פֶּסַח
דְּלָתָיו דָּפַקְתָּ כְּחֹם הַיּוֹם בַּפֶּסַח.
הִסְעִיד נוֹצְצִים עֻגוֹת מַצּוֹת בַּפֶּסַח.
וְאֶל הַבָּקָר רָץ זֵכֶר לְשׁוֹר עֵרֶךְ פֶּסַח.
וַאֲמַרְתֶּם זֶבַח פֶּסַח
זֹעֲמוּ סְדוֹמִים וְלוֹהֲטוּ בָּאֵשׁ בַּפֶּסַח.
חֻלַּץ לוֹט מֵהֶם וּמַצּוֹת אָפָה בְּקֵץ בַּפֶּסַח.
טֵאטֵאתָ אַדְמַת מוֹף וְנוֹף בְּעָבְרְךָ בַּפֶּסַח.
וַאֲמַרְתֶּם זֶבַח פֶּסַח
יָהּ רֹאשׁ כָּל אוֹן מָחַצְתָּ בְּלֵיל שִׁמּוּר בַּפֶּסַח.
כַּבִּיר עַל בֵּן בְּכוֹר פָּסַחְתָּ בְּדַם בַּפֶּסַח.
לְבִלְתִּי תֵת מַשְׁחִית לָבֹא בִפְתָחַי בַּפֶּסַח.
וַאֲמַרְתֶּם זֶבַח פֶּסַח

מִסְגֶּרֶת סֻגְּרָה בְּעִתּוֹתֵי פֶּסַח
נִשְׁמְדָה מִדְיָן בִּצְלִיל שְׂעוֹרֵי עֹמֶר פֶּסַח
שֹׂרְפוּ מִשְׁמַנֵּי פּוּל וְלוּד בִּיקַד יְקוֹדפֶּסַח
וַאֲמַרְתֶּם זֶבַח פֶּסַח
עוֹד הַיּוֹם בְּנֹב לַעֲמוֹד עַד גָּעָה עוֹנַת פֶּסַח
פַּס יַד כָּתְבָה לְקַעֲקֵעַ צוּל פֶּסַח
צָפֹה הַצָּפִית עָרוֹךְ הַשֻּׁלְחָן פֶּסַח
וַאֲמַרְתֶּם זֶבַח פֶּסַח
קָהָל כִּנְּסָה הֲדַסָּה צוֹם לְשַׁלֵּשׁ בַּפֶּסַח
רֹאשׁ מִבֵּית רָשָׁע מָחַצְתָּ בְּעֵץ חֲמִשִּׁים פֶּסַח
שְׁתֵּי אֵלֶּה רֶגַע תָּבִיא לְעוּצִית פֶּסַח
תָּעֹז יָדְךָ וְתָרוּם יְמִינְךָ כְּלֵיל הִתְקַדֶּשׁ חַג פֶּסַח
וַאֲמַרְתֶּם זֶבַח פֶּסַח

III. TO HIM PRAISE IS DUE; TO HIM PRAISE IS FITTING

Powerful is the reign of the King; clearly distinguished from all others: And His angels say, "To You and only You; to You and again to You; to You, just You; to You God is kingship."   To Him praise is due; to Him praise is fitting.

Supreme is the reign of the King; crystal clear: And his loyal people say to Him, "To You and only You; to You and again to You; to You, just You; to You God is kingship."   To Him praise is due; to Him praise is fitting.

So worthy is the reign of the King; so mighty: And His angels say, "To You and only You; to You and again to You; to You, just You; to You God is kingship."   To Him praise is due; to Him praise is fitting.

Unique is the reign of the King; absolutely powerful: And His scholars say, "To You and only You; to You and again to You; to You, just You; to You God is kingship."   To Him praise is due; to Him praise is fitting.

The reign of the King is the only true reign; perfectly wondrous: And His angels say, "To You and only You; to You and again to You; to You, just You; to You God is kingship." To Him praise is due; to Him praise is fitting.

Yet humble is the reign of the King; He is the Redeemer: And his righteous people say, "To You and only You; to You and again to You; to You, just You; to You God is kingship." To Him praise is due; to Him praise is fitting.

Holy is the reign of the King; perfectly merciful: And His angels say, "To You and only You; to You and again to You; to You, just You; to You God is kingship." To Him praise is due; to Him praise is fitting.

Mighty is the reign of the King; always giving support: And His pure people say, "To You and only You; to You and again to You; to You, just You; to You God is kingship." To Him praise is due; to Him praise is fitting.

כִּי לוֹ נָאֶה. כִּי לוֹ יָאֶה:

אַדִּיר בִּמְלוּכָה. בָּחוּר כַּהֲלָכָה. גְּדוּדָיו יֹאמְרוּ לוֹ. לְךָ וּלְךָ. לְךָ כִּי לְךָ. לְךָ אַף לְךָ. לְךָ
יהוה הַמַּמְלָכָה. כִּי לוֹ נָאֶה. כִּי לוֹ יָאֶה:

דָּגוּל בִּמְלוּכָה. הָדוּר כַּהֲלָכָה. וָתִיקָיו יֹאמְרוּ לוֹ. לְךָ וּלְךָ. לְךָ כִּי לְךָ. לְךָ אַף לְךָ. לְךָ
יהוה הַמַּמְלָכָה. כִּי לוֹ נָאֶה. כִּי לוֹ יָאֶה:

זַכַּאי בִּמְלוּכָה. חָסִין כַּהֲלָכָה. טַפְסְרָיו יֹאמְרוּ לוֹ. לְךָ וּלְךָ. לְךָ כִּי לְךָ. לְךָ אַף לְךָ.
לְךָ יהוה הַמַּמְלָכָה. כִּי לוֹ נָאֶה. כִּי לוֹ יָאֶה:

יָחִיד בִּמְלוּכָה. כַּבִּיר כַּהֲלָכָה. סְבִיבָיו יֹאמְרוּ לוֹ. לְךָ וּלְךָ. לְךָ כִּי לְךָ. לְךָ אַף לְךָ.
לְךָ יהוה הַמַּמְלָכָה. כִּי לוֹ נָאֶה. כִּי לוֹ יָאֶה:

מֶלֶךְ בִּמְלוּכָה. נוֹרָא כַּהֲלָכָה. סְבִיבָיו יֹאמְרוּ לוֹ. לְךָ וּלְךָ. לְךָ כִּי לְךָ. לְךָ אַף לְךָ.
לְךָ יהוה הַמַּמְלָכָה. כִּי לוֹ נָאֶה. כִּי לוֹ יָאֶה:

עָנָו בִּמְלוּכָה. פּוֹדֶה כַּהֲלָכָה. צַדִּיקָיו יֹאמְרוּ לוֹ. לְךָ וּלְךָ. לְךָ כִּי לְךָ. לְךָ אַף לְךָ. לְךָ
יהוה הַמַּמְלָכָה. כִּי לוֹ נָאֶה. כִּי לוֹ יָאֶה:

קָדוֹשׁ בִּמְלוּכָה. רַחוּם כַּהֲלָכָה. שִׁנְאַנָּיו יֹאמְרוּ לוֹ. לְךָ וּלְךָ. לְךָ כִּי לְךָ. לְךָ אַף לְךָ.
לְךָ יהוה הַמַּמְלָכָה. כִּי לוֹ נָאֶה. כִּי לוֹ יָאֶה:

תַּקִּיף בִּמְלוּכָה. תּוֹמֵךְ כַּהֲלָכָה. תְּמִימָיו יֹאמְרוּ לוֹ. לְךָ וּלְךָ. לְךָ כִּי לְךָ. לְךָ אַף לְךָ.
לְךָ יהוה הַמַּמְלָכָה. כִּי לוֹ נָאֶה. כִּי לוֹ יָאֶה:

IV. HE IS MIGHTY

He is mighty. May He soon rebuild the Temple; His house. Speedily; very speedily, and soon, in our lifetime. God rebuild; God, rebuild; rebuild Your house soon.

He is excellence. He is great. He is transcendent. May He soon rebuild the Temple; His house. Speedily; very speedily, and soon, in our lifetime. God rebuild; God, rebuild; rebuild Your house soon.

He is beauty. He is truth. He is pure. He is righteousness. May He soon rebuild the Temple; His house. Speedily; very speedily, and soon, in our lifetime. God rebuild; God, rebuild; rebuild Your house soon.

He is pristine. He is unique. He is grandeur. He is the source of wisdom. He is king. He is awesome. He is strength. He is all-powerful. He redeems. May He soon rebuild the Temple; His house. Speedily; very speedily, and soon, in our lifetime. God rebuild; God, rebuild; rebuild Your house soon.

He is holy. He is merciful. He is the Almighty. He is the source of all power. May He soon rebuild the Temple; His house. Speedily; very speedily, and soon, in our lifetime. God rebuild; God, rebuild; rebuild Your house soon.

אַדִּיר הוּא

אַדִּיר הוּא יִבְנֶה בֵיתוֹ בְּקָרוֹב, בִּמְהֵרָה בְּיָמֵינוּ בְּקָרוֹב. אֵל בְּנֵה אֵל בְּנֵה בְּנֵה בֵיתְךָ בְּקָרוֹב.

בָּחוּר הוּא, גָּדוֹל הוּא, דָּגוּל הוּא, יִבְנֶה בֵיתוֹ בְּקָרוֹב, בִּמְהֵרָה, בְּיָמֵינוּ בְּקָרוֹב. אֵל בְּנֵה אֵל בְּנֵה בְּנֵה בֵיתְךָ בְּקָרוֹב.

הָדוּר הוּא, וָתִיק הוּא, זַכַּאי הוּא, חָסִיד הוּא, יִבְנֶה בֵיתוֹ בְּקָרוֹב. בִּמְהֵרָה בְּיָמֵינוּ בְּקָרוֹב. אֵל בְּנֵה בְּנֵה בֵיתְךָ בְּקָרוֹב.

טָהוֹר הוּא, יָחִיד הוּא, כַּבִּיר הוּא, לָמוּד הוּא, מֶלֶךְ הוּא, נוֹרָא הוּא, סַגִּיב הוּא, עִזּוּז הוּא, פּוֹדֶה הוּא, צַדִּיק הוּא יִבְנֶה בֵיתוֹ בְּקָרוֹב. בִּמְהֵרָה בְּיָמֵינוּ בְּקָרוֹב. אֵל בְּנֵה אֵל בְּנֵה בְּנֵה בֵיתְךָ בְּקָרוֹב.

קָדוֹשׁ הוּא, רַחוּם הוּא, שַׁדַּי הוּא, תַּקִּיף הוּא, יִבְנֶה בֵיתוֹ בְּקָרוֹב. בִּמְהֵרָה בְּיָמֵינוּ בְּקָרוֹב. אֵל בְּנֵה אֵל בְּנֵה בְּנֵה בֵיתְךָ בְּקָרוֹב.

V. WHO KNOWS ONE?

Who knows one? I know one! One is our God, in the heaven and on the earth.

Who knows two? I know two! Two are the tablets of the ten commandments; One is our God, in the heaven and on the earth.

Who knows three? I know three! Three are the fathers of the Jewish people. Two are the tablets of the ten commandments; One is our God, in the heaven and on the earth.

Who knows four? I know four! Four are the mothers of the Jewish people. Three are the fathers of the Jewish people. Two are the tablets of the ten commandments; One is our God, in the heaven and on the earth.

Who knows five? I know five! Five are the books of the Torah. Four are the mothers of the Jewish people. Three are the fathers of the Jewish people. Two are the tablets of the ten commandments; One is our God, in the heaven and on the earth.

Who knows six? I know six! Six are the sections of the mishnah. Five are the books of the Torah. Four are the mothers of the Jewish people. Three are the fathers of the Jewish people. Two are the tablets of the ten commandments; One is our God, in the heaven and on the earth.

Who knows seven? I know seven! Seven are the days of the week. Six are the sections of the mishnah. Five are the books of the Torah. Four are the mothers of the Jewish people. Three are the fathers of the Jewish people. Two are the tablets of the ten commandments; One is our God, in the heaven and on the earth.

Who knows eight? I know eight! Eight are the days before a circumcision. Seven are the days of the week. Six are the sections of the mishnah. Five are the books of the Torah. Four are the mothers of the Jewish people. Three are the fathers of the Jewish people. Two are the tablets of the ten commandments; One is our God, in the heaven and on the earth.

Who knows nine? I know nine! Nine are the months of pregnancy. Eight are the days before a circumcision. Seven are the days of the week. Six are the sections of the mishnah. Five are the books of the Torah. Four are the mothers of the Jewish people. Three are the fathers of the Jewish people. Two are the tablets of the ten commandments; One is our God, in the heaven and on the earth.

Who knows ten? I know ten! Ten are the ten commandments. Nine are the months of pregnancy. Eight are the days before a circumcision. Seven are the days of the week. Six are the sections of the mishnah. Five are the books of the Torah. Four are the mothers of the Jewish people. Three are the fathers of the Jewish people. Two are the tablets of the ten commandments; One is our God, in the heaven and on the earth.

Who knows eleven? I know eleven! Eleven are the stars from Joseph's dream. Ten are the ten commandments. Nine are the months of pregnancy. Eight are the days before a circumcision. Seven are the days of the week. Six are the sections of the mishnah. Five are the books of the Torah. Four are the mothers of the Jewish people. Three are the fathers of the Jewish people. Two are the tablets of the ten commandments; One is our God, in the heaven and on the earth.

Who knows twelve? I know twelve! Twelve are Jacob's sons, the tribes of Israel. Eleven are the stars from Joseph's dream. Ten are the ten commandments. Nine are the months of pregnancy. Eight are the days before a circumcision. Seven are the days of the week. Six are the sections of the mishnah. Five are the books of the Torah. Four are the mothers of the Jewish people. Three are the fathers of the Jewish people. Two are the tablets of the ten commandments; One is our God, in the heaven and on the earth.

Who knows thirteen? I know thirteen! Thirteen are the thirteen attributes of God's mercy. Twelve are Jacob's sons, the tribes of Israel. Eleven are the stars from Joseph's dream. Ten are the ten commandments. Nine are the months of pregnancy. Eight are the days before a circumcision. Seven are the days of the week. Six are the sections of the mishnah. Five are the books of the Torah. Four are the mothers of the Jewish people. Three are the fathers of the Jewish people. Two are the tablets of the ten commandments; One is our God, in the heaven and on the earth.

אֶחָד מִי יוֹדֵעַ. אֶחָד אֲנִי יוֹדֵעַ. אֶחָד אֱלֹהֵנוּ שֶׁבַּשָּׁמַיִם וּבָאָרֶץ.

שְׁנַיִם מִי יוֹדֵעַ. שְׁנַיִם אֲנִי יוֹדֵעַ. שְׁנֵי לֻחוֹת הַבְּרִית. אֶחָד אֱלֹהֵנוּ שֶׁבַּשָּׁמַיִם וּבָאָרֶץ.

שְׁלֹשָׁה מִי יוֹדֵעַ. שְׁלֹשָׁה אֲנִי יוֹדֵעַ. שְׁלֹשָׁה אָבוֹת. שְׁנֵי לֻחוֹת הַבְּרִית. אֶחָד אֱלֹהֵנוּ שֶׁבַּשָּׁמַיִם וּבָאָרֶץ.

אַרְבַּע מִי יוֹדֵעַ. אַרְבַּע אֲנִי יוֹדֵעַ. אַרְבַּע אִמָּהוֹת. שְׁלֹשָׁה אָבוֹת. שְׁנֵי לֻחוֹת הַבְּרִית. אֶחָד אֱלֹהֵנוּ שֶׁבַּשָּׁמַיִם וּבָאָרֶץ.

חֲמִשָּׁה מִי יוֹדֵעַ. חֲמִשָּׁה אֲנִי יוֹדֵעַ. חֲמִשָּׁה חֻמְשֵׁי תוֹרָה. אַרְבַּע אִמָּהוֹת. שְׁלֹשָׁה אָבוֹת. שְׁנֵי לֻחוֹת הַבְּרִית. אֶחָד אֱלֹהֵנוּ שֶׁבַּשָּׁמַיִם וּבָאָרֶץ.

שִׁשָּׁה מִי יוֹדֵעַ. שִׁשָּׁה אֲנִי יוֹדֵעַ. שִׁשָּׁה סִדְרֵי מִשְׁנָה. חֲמִשָּׁה חֻמְשֵׁי תוֹרָה. אַרְבַּע אִמָּהוֹת. שְׁלֹשָׁה אָבוֹת. שְׁנֵי לֻחוֹת הַבְּרִית. אֶחָד אֱלֹהֵנוּ שֶׁבַּשָּׁמַיִם וּבָאָרֶץ.

שִׁבְעָה מִי יוֹדֵעַ. שִׁבְעָה אֲנִי יוֹדֵעַ. שִׁבְעָה יְמֵי שַׁבַּתָּה. שִׁשָּׁה סִדְרֵי מִשְׁנָה. חֲמִשָּׁה חֻמְשֵׁי תוֹרָה. אַרְבַּע אִמָּהוֹת. שְׁלֹשָׁה אָבוֹת. שְׁנֵי לֻחוֹת הַבְּרִית. אֶחָד אֱלֹהֵנוּ שֶׁבַּשָּׁמַיִם וּבָאָרֶץ.

שְׁמוֹנָה מִי יוֹדֵעַ. שְׁמוֹנָה אֲנִי יוֹדֵעַ. שְׁמוֹנָה יְמֵי מִילָה. שִׁבְעָה יְמֵי שַׁבַּתָּה. שִׁשָּׁה סִדְרֵי מִשְׁנָה. חֲמִשָּׁה חֻמְשֵׁי תוֹרָה. אַרְבַּע אִמָּהוֹת. שְׁלֹשָׁה אָבוֹת. שְׁנֵי לֻחוֹת הַבְּרִית. אֶחָד אֱלֹהֵנוּ שֶׁבַּשָּׁמַיִם וּבָאָרֶץ.

תִּשְׁעָה מִי יוֹדֵעַ. תִּשְׁעָה אֲנִי יוֹדֵעַ. תִּשְׁעָה יַרְחֵי לֵדָה. שְׁמוֹנָה יְמֵי מִילָה. שִׁבְעָה יְמֵי
שַׁבַּתָּה. שִׁשָּׁה סִדְרֵי מִשְׁנָה. חֲמִשָּׁה חֻמְשֵׁי תוֹרָה. אַרְבַּע אִמָּהוֹת. שְׁלֹשָׁה אָבוֹת. שְׁנֵי לֻחוֹת
הַבְּרִית. אֶחָד אֱלֹהֵינוּ שֶׁבַּשָּׁמַיִם וּבָאָרֶץ.

עֲשָׂרָה מִי יוֹדֵעַ. עֲשָׂרָה אֲנִי יוֹדֵעַ. עֲשָׂרָה דִבְּרַיָּא. תִּשְׁעָה יַרְחֵי לֵדָה. שְׁמוֹנָה יְמֵי מִילָה.
שִׁבְעָה יְמֵי שַׁבַּתָּה. שִׁשָּׁה סִדְרֵי מִשְׁנָה. חֲמִשָּׁה חֻמְשֵׁי תוֹרָה. אַרְבַּע אִמָּהוֹת. שְׁלֹשָׁה אָבוֹת.
שְׁנֵי לֻחוֹת הַבְּרִית. אֶחָד אֱלֹהֵינוּ שֶׁבַּשָּׁמַיִם וּבָאָרֶץ.

אַחַד עָשָׂר מִי יוֹדֵעַ. אַחַד עָשָׂר אֲנִי יוֹדֵעַ. אַחַד עָשָׂר כּוֹכְבַיָּא. עֲשָׂרָה דִבְּרַיָּא. תִּשְׁעָה יַרְחֵי
לֵדָה. שְׁמוֹנָה יְמֵי מִילָה. שִׁבְעָה יְמֵי שַׁבַּתָּה. שִׁשָּׁה סִדְרֵי מִשְׁנָה. חֲמִשָּׁה חֻמְשֵׁי תוֹרָה. אַרְבַּע
אִמָּהוֹת. שְׁלֹשָׁה אָבוֹת. שְׁנֵי לֻחוֹת הַבְּרִית. אֶחָד אֱלֹהֵינוּ שֶׁבַּשָּׁמַיִם וּבָאָרֶץ.

שְׁנֵים עָשָׂר מִי יוֹדֵעַ. שְׁנֵים עָשָׂר אֲנִי יוֹדֵעַ. שְׁנֵים עָשָׂר שִׁבְטַיָּא. אַחַד עָשָׂר כּוֹכְבַיָּא.
עֲשָׂרָה דִבְּרַיָּא. תִּשְׁעָה יַרְחֵי לֵדָה. שְׁמוֹנָה יְמֵי מִילָה. שִׁבְעָה יְמֵי שַׁבַּתָּה. שִׁשָּׁה סִדְרֵי מִשְׁנָה.
חֲמִשָּׁה חֻמְשֵׁי תוֹרָה. אַרְבַּע אִמָּהוֹת. שְׁלֹשָׁה אָבוֹת. שְׁנֵי לֻחוֹת הַבְּרִית. אֶחָד אֱלֹהֵינוּ
שֶׁבַּשָּׁמַיִם וּבָאָרֶץ.

שְׁלֹשָׁה עָשָׂר מִי יוֹדֵעַ. שְׁלֹשָׁה עָשָׂר אֲנִי יוֹדֵעַ. שְׁלֹשָׁה עָשָׂר מִדַּיָּא. שְׁנֵים עָשָׂר שִׁבְטַיָּא.
אַחַד עָשָׂר כּוֹכְבַיָּא. עֲשָׂרָה דִבְּרַיָּא. תִּשְׁעָה יַרְחֵי לֵדָה. שְׁמוֹנָה יְמֵי מִילָה. שִׁבְעָה יְמֵי שַׁבַּתָּה.
שִׁשָּׁה סִדְרֵי מִשְׁנָה. חֲמִשָּׁה חֻמְשֵׁי תוֹרָה. אַרְבַּע אִמָּהוֹת. שְׁלֹשָׁה אָבוֹת. שְׁנֵי לֻחוֹת הַבְּרִית.
אֶחָד אֱלֹהֵינוּ שֶׁבַּשָּׁמַיִם וּבָאָרֶץ.

VI. ONE KID

One kid goat, one kid; that father bought for two zuzim, one kid, one kid.

And then a cat came and ate the kid; that father bought for two zuzim, one kid, one kid.

And then a dog came and bit the cat that ate the kid; that father bought for two zuzim, one kid, one kid.

And then a stick came and hit the dog, that bit the cat, that ate the kid; that father bought for two zuzim, one kid, one kid.

And then fire came and burned the stick that hit the dog, that bit the cat that ate the kid; that father bought for two zuzim, one kid, one kid.

And then water and doused the fire, that burned the stick, that hit the dog, that bit the cat, that ate the kid; that father bought for two zuzim, one kid, one kid.

And then an ox came and drank the water that doused the fire, that burned the stick, that hit the dog, that bit the cat, that ate the kid; that father bought for two zuzim, one kid, one kid.

And then came the shochet (ritual slaughterer) and slaughtered the ox, that drank the water, that doused the fire, that burned the stick, that hit the dog, that bit the cat, that ate the kid; that father bought for two zuzim, one kid, one kid.

And then came the Angel of Death and killed the shochet that slaughtered the ox, that drank the water, that doused the fire, that burned the stick, that hit the dog, that bit the cat, that ate the kid; that father bought for two zuzim, one kid, one kid.

חַד גַּדְיָא, חַד גַּדְיָא, דְּזַבִּין אַבָּא בִּתְרֵי זוּזֵי, חַד גַּדְיָא חַד גַּדְיָא.

וְאָתָא שׁוּנְרָא וְאָכְלָה לְגַדְיָא, דְּזַבִּין אַבָּא בִּתְרֵי זוּזֵי, חַד גַּדְיָא חַד גַּדְיָא.

וְאָתָא כַלְבָּא וְנָשַׁךְ לְשׁוּנְרָא, דְּאָכְלָה לְגַדְיָא, דְּזַבִּין אַבָּא בִּתְרֵי זוּזֵי, חַד גַּדְיָא חַד גַּדְיָא.

וְאָתָא חוּטְרָא וְהִכָּה לְכַלְבָּא, דְּנָשַׁךְ לְשׁוּנְרָא, דְּאָכְלָה לְגַדְיָא, דְּזַבִּין אַבָּא בִּתְרֵי זוּזֵי, חַד גַּדְיָא חַד גַּדְיָא.

וְאָתָא נוּרָא וְשָׂרַף לְחוּטְרָא, דְּהִכָּה לְכַלְבָּא, דְּנָשַׁךְ לְשׁוּנְרָא, דְּאָכְלָה לְגַדְיָא, דְּזַבִּין אַבָּא בִּתְרֵי זוּזֵי, חַד גַּדְיָא.

וְאָתָא מַיָּא וְכָבָה לְנוּרָא, דְּשָׂרַף לְחוּטְרָא, דְּהִכָּה לְכַלְבָּא, דְּנָשַׁךְ לְשׁוּנְרָא, דְּאָכְלָה לְגַדְיָא, דְּזַבִּין אַבָּא בִּתְרֵי זוּזֵי, חַד גַּדְיָא חַד גַּדְיָא.

וְאָתָא תוֹרָא וְשָׁתָה לְמַיָּא, דְּכָבָה לְנוּרָא, דְּשָׂרַף לְחוּטְרָא, דְּהִכָּה לְכַלְבָּא, דְּנָשַׁךְ לְשׁוּנְרָא, דְּאָכְלָה לְגַדְיָא, דְּזַבִּין אַבָּא בִּתְרֵי זוּזֵי, חַד גַּדְיָא חַד גַּדְיָא.

וְאָתָא הַשׁוֹחֵט וְשָׁחַט לְתוֹרָא, דְּשָׁתָה לְמַיָּא, דְּכָבָה לְנוּרָא, דְּשָׂרַף לְחוּטְרָא, דְּהִכָּה לְכַלְבָּא, דְּנָשַׁךְ לְשׁוּנְרָא, דְּאָכְלָה לְגַדְיָא, דְּזַבִּין אַבָּא בִּתְרֵי זוּזֵי, חַד גַּדְיָא חַד גַּדְיָא.

וְאָתָא מַלְאַךְ הַמָּוֶת וְשָׁחַט לְשׁוֹחֵט, דְּשָׁחַט לְתוֹרָא, דְּשָׁתָה לְמַיָּא, דְּכָבָה לְנוּרָא, דְּשָׂרַף לְחוּטְרָא, דְּהִכָּה לְכַלְבָּא, דְּנָשַׁךְ לְשׁוּנְרָא, דְּאָכְלָה לְגַדְיָא, דְּזַבִּין אַבָּא בִּתְרֵי זוּזֵי, חַד גַּדְיָא חַד גַּדְיָא.

וְאָתָא הַקָּדוֹשׁ בָּרוּךְ הוּא וְשָׁחַט לְמַלְאַךְ הַמָּוֶת, דְּשָׁחַט לְשׁוֹחֵט, דְּשָׁחַט לְתוֹרָא, דְּשָׁתָה לְמַיָּא, דְּכָבָה לְנוּרָא, דְּשָׂרַף לְחוּטְרָא, דְּהִכָּה לְכַלְבָּא, דְּנָשַׁךְ לְשׁוּנְרָא, דְּאָכְלָה לְגַדְיָא, דְּזַבִּין אַבָּא בִּתְרֵי זוּזֵי, חַד גַּדְיָא חַד גַּדְיָא.

We did it!
We did it!
We finished the whole Haggadah.
From all the Matzahbreis; have a
great Passover, a great year, a great
nights sleep; and we'll see you next
year—In Jerusalem!

LEVIATHAN PRESS
BOOKS THAT MAKE A DIFFERENCE

AVAILABLE NOW

ROSH HASHANAH YOM KIPPUR SURVIVAL KIT
by Shimon Apisdorf
Bestselling recipient of a Benjamin Franklin Award.
There you are; it's the middle of High Holy Day services, and frankly, you're confused. Enter—the *Rosh Hashanah Yom Kippur Survival Kit*. This book follows the order of the services and masterfully blends wisdom, humor and down-to-earth spirituality. It's like having a knowledgeable friend sitting right next to you in synagogue.

THE ONE HOUR PURIM PRIMER
by Shimon Apisdorf
This book contains everything a family needs to understand, celebrate and enjoy Purim. Whether you have celebrated Purim fifty times or never at all; this book has something for everyone. It combines a clear, step-by-step guide to the holiday with lucid insights that reveal how Purim speaks to our lives today.

PASSOVER SURVIVAL KIT
by Shimon Apisdorf
This internationally acclaimed bestseller, serves as a friendly gateway through which you will enter the world of Passover and see it as you have never seen it before. The *Passover Survival Kit* enables you to experience one of the center-pieces of Jewish life as insightful, thought provoking and relevant to issues of personal growth and the everyday challenges of life. This book stands on it's own and also serves as a companion volume to *The Survival Kit Family Haggadah*.

New For 1997

Spring '97

THE DEATH OF CUPID: RECLAIMING THE WISDOM OF LOVE, DATING, ROMANCE AND MARRIAGE
by Nachum Braverman & Shimon Apisdorf
The Death of Cupid is divided into four sections: The Wisdom of Marriage, The Wisdom of Dating, The Wisdom of Sex and The Wisdom of Romance. This book speaks equally to singles in search of love and couples seeking to deepen their relationship.

Summer '97

MISSILES, MASKS AND MIRACLES
by Charles Samuel
The astonishing true account of the invisible shield protecting Israel during the Gulf War. Operation Desert Storm. The world watched: Israel prepared it's population for thousands of casualties; Scud missiles destroyed thousands of homes and amazingly, only one person was killed.
"The Prime Minister visited the area with the mayor of Tel Aviv. Mr. Shamir asked if in fact there had been people in the shelter at the time of the attack. The mayor replied that there had been two hundred, and all were saved by a miracle."

Fall '97

CHANUKAH REVIVAL KIT
by Shimon Apisdorf
This book takes you way beyond the wrapping paper to discover a little known spiritual dimension of Chanukah. From the lighting of the candles to the dreidel to the Maccabees; this book explores fascinating dimensions of this popular holiday. Great gift, ideal for families.

About the Author

Shimon Apisdorf is an award-winning author whose books have been read by hundreds of thousands of people all over the world. Shimon has gained a world-wide reputation for his ability to extract the essence of classical Jewish wisdom and show how it can be relevant to the essential issues facing the mind, heart and soul in today's world. His writings speak poignantly, with rare sensitivity and with humor to people of all backgrounds. Shimon grew up in Cleveland, Ohio and attended the University of Cincinnati, Telshe Yeshiva and Yeshivat Aish HaTorah in Jerusalem where he received rabbinic ordination. He currently resides with his wife and children in Baltimore. The Apisdorfs enjoy taking long walks, feeding the ducks and going to Orioles games. As for the Ravens: Forget it! You can reach Shimon at: ShimonA@mail.idt.net.